Hour of the Beaver

Hour of the Beaver

illustrated with photographs

HOPE SAWYER BUYUKMIHCI

RAND M^CNALLY & COMPANY   Chicago   New York   San Francisco

The photographs on pages 40, 48, 53, 56,
67, 72, 92, 99, 136, 144, 164, and front
jacket by Alfred A. Francesconi; on page 60
and back jacket by Cavit Buyukmihci; all
others by the author

Copyright © 1971 by Hope Sawyer Buyukmihci
All rights reserved
Library of Congress Catalog Card Number:
  78-146290
Printed in the United States of America
by Rand McNally & Company
First printing, August, 1971

In memory of Grey Owl,
who lured me along the trail

Sharpen your wits when you observe man and nature—
because understanding the unique strength and beauty within
all living things is the heart of happiness.

JUNE CALLWOOD

CONTENTS

ILLUSTRATIONS

Hour of the
Beaver

THE BEAVER HOUR

By
Hope Sawyer Buyukmihci

Between the dark and the daylight,
When the dusk is beginning to lower,
Comes a pause in the day's occupation
Which is known as The Beaver Hour.

Then from the town and village,
And sometimes from cities afar,
The beaver-watchers come trekking —
By foot, by bike and by car.

They take their seat in the twilight
With a poplar twig in each hand
And quietly wait eyes shining,
For the furry beaver band.

A little beaver swims shoreward,
And waddles up on the land,
To take with delicate fingers
A twig from a child's hand.

He pauses a grateful moment,
Then glides away with his prize
Leaving a happy youngster
With sparkling, fun-filled eyes.

Beaver Hour brings together
Creatures of different name;
Different looks and different ways,
But love of life the same.

All little woodland creatures
Want to be friends with man;
Kindness and patience are all it takes —
If we want to be friends, we can.

Adventure Trail

PUTTING ON old work gloves, I took down the clippers from their hook in the barn and whistled to our dog Junior. He was as eager as I to investigate the New Jersey woodland which my husband and I had just set aside as a sanctuary for wildlife—and as a 250-acre studio where I could study and sketch animals in their natural habitat.

Junior's urge to chase was strong, but he had gradually curbed it to a brisk curiosity which no longer needed the fillip of the chase. He had developed into a sort of canine naturalist and was a joy to have along.

As we walked the path to the woods this November day, sassafras, maple, and gum leaves danced in the crisp breeze, which pressed against the hair on Junior's chest and filtered through the backs of my cotton gloves. Early snow had fallen, blanketing green grass, frosting leaves, and making stiffened ghosts of wild asters.

From behind the oaks east of the cabin the sun blazed. A flock of eight ducks passed over us. Rustling like a gust of driven leaves, they whirled erratically and whisked into the water of the pond, while a woodcock flapped overhead like a large bat, his wings whistling.

Fifteen Canada geese drifted on the pond, most with their heads tucked underwing. Wildfowl hunting season had begun, and daily we heard shots. Ponds outside the refuge were ringed with camouflaged hunters. This small flock, escaping volleys of gunfire, had fled in haphazard formation to drop into our pond, where they stayed warily on the far side. While they floated, sleeping, one of them kept guard, his regal black-and-white head held high.

I stood for a moment to watch them. Suddenly each tucked head emerged from under its wing, and the whole flock rose abruptly, climbed into the sky, and disappeared over the woods to the south. There they would feed in our neighbor's field of greens.

These were wild geese, noble birds who mate for life. Their kind used to be abundant from Labrador to Tennessee, and their nests were common in our Midwest. Now their nests are mostly in inaccessible places in the northland, hidden in sedge, in low bushes, or even among lower branches of trees. Perhaps these particular geese had nested on top of beaver lodges, which would provide them with a moat and a lookout point at the same time.

I looked at the deserted beaver lodge in the middle of our pond. When we first came, we found a rusted trap still unsprung on top of it. Seeing the empty lodge crumbling away, I imagined a wild gander standing there alert, ready to defend his goose while she sat for a month on her eggs. I pictured the gander's snaky neck thrust out, serrated beak open, his powerful wings with their nearly six-foot spread ready to flail any enemy who might threaten. The eggs would have hatched in June, fluffy olive-yellow goslings stepping out like gawky, outsize ducklings dipped in smoke.

Until now this present flock had survived the threats to the wild goose: widespread drainage of marshlands, unnatural harvest of wild rice as "status food" for humans, persecution by farmers because of destruction to crops. I wished I could convince our neighbor that the invasion of his crop by the geese meant not just the eating of green leaves, but valuable insect control as well. But crop damage was only an excuse. If necessary, he would have planted a crop purposely to lure the geese within gunshot.

Junior and I had barely reached the woods when several guns boomed from the direction of the mustard field and the ragged remnant of the flock came winging back to make a splashy, disorganized landing. Counting beaks, I found only twelve. Stay here! I begged them silently, but I knew they would return to the green feast daily until no geese remained. It had happened before.

Unexpected Wildlife Refuge is a narrow corridor between a sparsely inhabited area on the east, farmland on the south and west, and heavily hunted forest bordering the north side. In establishing the refuge we had put ourselves in the cross fire of sport hunting, traditional farming, and wholesale upheaval of nature by "progress." All wild animals face this problem, and in taking their part we were in it too.

My dream of a refuge had taken shape while we were living in Turkey. There, contrasts which had been more or less hidden from my experience in America stared me in the face. Perhaps my father's being a naturalist had something to do with my reaction. And surely my position as wife of a Moslem gave me new insight into the plight of oppressed creatures. (An oft-quoted Moslem proverb declares that heaven for a woman is under her husband's foot.)

My own struggle for independence in a culture where women were regarded as playthings, ornaments, or slaves intensified my sympathy for supposedly lesser beings suffering under the domination of mankind; and I was outraged at both Turks and Americans who, intent on their own comfort and prestige, apparently had no thought for the way animals were treated.

Working for the United States government, I became caught up in the tinsel of embassy life and the raw competition for civil-service ratings. But despite my busy schedule, I had time to observe the life around me. And the more I saw, the more discouraged I became. Everywhere I saw donkeys overloaded until they fell on the harsh cobbles; skinny horses whipped uphill; limp strings of quail brought in by Americans who gloated, "They're so tame you can knock 'em over with a stick."

Nobody seemed to care. When I told Cavit, my husband, how I felt, he sympathized; but like most Moslems, he bowed to Allah's will. I could not bow, and I could not adjust. More and more the sound of blows striking donkeys' hides and the sight of lambs being led through the street to slaughter hurt me.

Yet I had not the courage to stand up for animals. All I could do was dream of escape, escape back to America where our three children could live unexposed to the kind of cruelty I saw all around me. I did not realize then how much my outlook was colored by homesickness, and I had completely forgotten that there was unconcern, as well as cruelty, at home.

After five years, we returned to America—Cavit as an immigrant to the land of his student days and I to my own country, whose ground I could have knelt down to kiss. I had long shared the feelings of banished ones who carried with them a little bag of native soil like a talisman.

By that time my dream and my husband's were one: an abandoned farm on the slope of Mount Baker in Washington, where a rollicking brook sparkled and bears came down to eat windfalls under old orchard trees. We had spent our honeymoon there. Cavit, like me, had a farm background, and he shared my regard for the beauties of nature. Together we envisioned a place with horses for the children to ride, a bountiful garden, and wild animals all around us.

But we reached New York with three youngsters and only a few dollars in our pocket. Even I had to bow to Allah's will and modify my dream. After a sojourn in a friend's trailer in southern New Jersey, we settled for an old farmhouse on three acres of land with neither woods nor water. There the children had a dog and a host of other pets, and I became aware of the difficulties both children and animals face in the country I love.

It was by allying ourselves with our children that Cavit and I developed a determination to stand up for animals. Our children taught us by leading us to questions we had never thought to ask.

"Why do they kill a frog for every student?" our son Ned had asked when he entered biology class. We had him excused from dissection.

"We can't let her die," declared Linda when one of our dogs was so far gone with distemper that we considered putting her away. She recovered under expensive treatment.

As for Nermin, our youngest, her love for animals swayed us to a vegetarian diet when we finally faced the subject of meat eating, which so troubles many children until they have become hardened to it.

I found our children eager to learn about natural history. They asked me to speak about nature to their classmates, and it was through contact with schoolchildren that I found out that animals were still being classified as varmints, targets, or pelts. It became plain why our rambles in the surrounding countryside did not reveal the wealth of wildlife we had expected.

The realization that our children had never seen a bluebird made me decide that we must have more than three acres on which to erect nesting boxes and provide a habitat safe from encroaching bulldozers. We ended up with a 250-acre tract of woods and water, acquired by luck and debt; and we named it Unexpected Wildlife Refuge after Unexpected Road, on which it is located.

Immediately we began making birdhouses, and we spent every weekend at the refuge while planning how to remodel the old cabin into living quarters.

Junior and I were headed for Adventure Trail, far upstream from the pond, to a place where I had seen beaver tracks, and in the weeds along the shore, had found freshly peeled sticks. My great hope was that I might surprise a beaver, maybe even catch him at work cutting a tree. I was too ignorant to know how slim were my chances of spying on a beaver at work, though I had heard distant gnawing, and at times, the slap of a beaver's tail as he dived into the water.

After a quarter of a mile, Junior and I came to the wall of thick brush and greenbriers where I had stopped cutting the week before. I started in again, clearing a path. At the first click of the clippers the little dog wagged his tail, looked about like a small boy eager to help, then started biting off twigs with his teeth.

For an hour we labored, opening a trail under tall pines and cedars next to the creek, which flowed silently among the bushes. An old cedar log jutted into the current, and I stepped on it, gripping a clump of alders with one hand. Peering ahead, I saw the dark water disappear around a bend, while from a distance came the tinkle of falls. The sound recalled streams I had known in my childhood in upstate New York.

Half an hour later I stood on a narrow dam which stretched across the creek, connecting tree to tree in a zigzag line. The water stood deeper above than below the dam, and the stream shimmered over it in melodious falls. I examined the dam closely. Nestled among the sticks and mud lay rotting logs, mossy and green. Some of the mud was fresh—big hunks grubbed out of the water and pushed forcefully into chinks between the sticks. At one side of the falls gurgled an eddy, with a leaning branch of ilex dipping red berries into the foam.

Wading to the middle of the dam, I jumped up and down on it. "Solid," I announced to Junior, who hung back whining. He did not like to get wet. Looking upstream, I spied a stick caught among blueberry bushes along the far shore. It gleamed white in the shadows. "They've been here," I gloated. I looked around carefully but could see no other sign of life.

Sun reached through the trees; laying my jacket near the dam,

I wiped sweat from my face, then went on hacking through the brush, while Junior roamed away into the forest. No need for a watch to tell when it was noon, for my inner clock was true. Backtracking the trail, I pulled a bean sandwich out of my pocket and sat near the dam to eat. As I bit into the thick bread, Junior hurtled through the brush and stood before me. His nose was as faithful as my inner clock. His tail wagged and his brown eyes gleamed.

"You don't like beans," I said, taking another bite. He cocked his head, black and tan ears alert, and a drop of moisture appeared at the corner of his mouth. "But you love bread and butter," I agreed, and breaking off chunks, fed them to him. "That's all," I said, dusting my hands when the bread was gone. But Junior kept his head cocked, eyes expectant. I leaned over, took the other sandwich from my pocket, and shared it too. Topping off lunch with a handful of oatmeal cookies, we both took a drink of water from the stream, then lay down for a nap.

Suddenly I started up. In my sleep I had heard a noise. There, high above us, a red squirrel chirred and barked, almost choking with indignation. He pounded the bark with both hind feet, loosening pieces which sprinkled down. Junior jumped up, and tipping his head, squinted upward at the squirrel.

"Come on," I told him. "Old Chatterbox has smelled the crumbs and can't wait for us to go so he can eat."

On among the pines, cedars, and swamp maples we progressed, clearing away just enough brush to make a slender lane. In the treetops I saw gray squirrels' nests, big and round as basketballs; and in bushes just above eye level, I found several nests of wood thrushes and catbirds, from which the young had long since flown. In one spot, when I knelt to expose a sweet-pepper root, I came upon the grass-lined cup of a Maryland yellowthroat's nest, formed in a hollow close to the root.

In another place my clippers just missed a fat and lethargic leopard frog, who had dug himself deep into the duff for his winter's sleep. His legs were folded tightly, denting his body, the way both frogs and toads package themselves for hibernation. Groggily he opened his eyes, making no move to escape, and regarded me as though saying, "Turn off the light and cover me back up. I want to sleep." I dug a new bed for him away from the path and tucked him under a blanket of leaves, where he would stay until spring.

The day's sun had melted the frost, and it felt very springlike. I had the feeling of nearing a goal. I then saw a cone of debris up ahead, piled around a clump of swamp maples. Branches were mixed with mud, roots, and sections of small logs. It was a beaver lodge, four feet high. Cautiously I approached, quite certain that I had found the home of the beavers whose tooth marks I had seen. But upon coming closer, I saw that the dried mud had crumbled away and portions of the sides had collapsed. The somber trees, dark-flowing water, and tangled shrubs were a dramatic stage setting, but the actors had packed up and gone. I felt the oppressive aura which surrounds a deserted house.

Then I came on a cluster of sweet-pepper stumps, each bearing fresh marks of teeth. The beavers had just been there! Shouldering the clippers, I hurried home along the cleared path, exultant, and burst into the house where Cavit and Ned sat at the kitchen table enjoying a late afternoon snack. With them was our neighbor old Mike Deflora, a cup of coffee before him.

"They're there!" I told Cavit, waving the clippers.

He ducked. "Watch it. Who's 'they'?" His green eyes looked stern.

"You know very well," I answered, laying the clippers down and reaching for a cup and saucer.

"You saw a beaver," Ned said with teen-age scorn. "That's all you talk about."

"No beaver," said Cavit. "A mouse, maybe?"

I poured myself a cup of coffee and then divulged the news: three stumps with fresh marks of teeth on them.

Female red squirrel

"Beavers?" Mike asked. "Them's awful things. Their teeth'll chop you to pieces." With a trembling hand he raised the cup to his lips and blew on his coffee. "We had 'em on our creek once, and I dynamited 'em out. Haven't seen none since."

"Did one ever attack you?" I asked.

"I never give 'em a chance," said the old man. "They're bad. They dam up the water. Flood you out. Did you ever see the teeth on 'em?"

Yes, I had seen a beaver's teeth. In the Adirondacks when I was ten, I visited friends who had a tame beaver, Paddy, living in a fenced pond. Paddy with his big orange front teeth had gently taken dog biscuits from my hand, chewed them up with a crunch, and begged for more. I described him to Mike.

"Oh, a tame beaver!" he scoffed. "Wild ones are vicious. If you find any, let me know. I've got a friend's a trapper. He'll get rid of 'em for you."

My thoughts flashed to the empty lodge on the pond. "Is there an open season on *beavers?*"

"Sure. Fur'll fetch a good price. If you want some fun, lay some traps along that stream there. Catch a passel of muskrats and maybe a beaver; might even get yourself a mink." He got up, saying, "I'll be gettin' on. Got my hound dogs to feed." He went out the door and climbed into his pickup.

As Mike's truck disappeared around the first bend in our drive, I went back in to where Cavit sat gazing into his empty cup. I poured more coffee and sat down. "What did he want?" I asked.

"Oh, just lonely, I guess. He was telling about the good old days when he used to hunt these bogs. Hinting around, to see if he could still do it." There was sternness in my husband's face. As a youth in Turkey, he too had been a hunter when shooting an animal meant meat for the pot.

"I wonder if *he* set that trap on top of the lodge," I said.

"Could be. But it might've been anybody. This place has been wide open for years."

We sipped our coffee, not saying much. Ned had retired to his den. I knew that Cavit was pondering, as I was, how many beavers were left and how we could protect them. The immediate question was: Would we ever see them?

The following Saturday, out in the woods early, I was pelted by cold rain. Junior vanished into the underbrush. While my boots squished through low spots in the trail, I traversed in a few minutes what had taken hours to clear the week before. As I neared the dam, I heard a light splash, and through the gloom under the cedars, caught sight of something moving just above it. Before I could tell what it was, a mighty force hit the surface, and water flew all over. The last ripple spent itself at the edge, and I waited for a head to poke up. Nothing appeared. But I knew that only a beaver would slap the water like that.

After the day's work I went home, drenched by the rain but filled with enthusiasm. Again I burst into the kitchen shouting, "Beavers!" The girls were making a cake, and Cavit was stopping a leak in the kitchen sink. All three listened politely to my story: "I was standing there when all of a sudden—Kah-*bloom*!—something hit the water. He didn't come up again, but I'm sure it was a beaver. How did he know I was there?"

I did not realize then how far superior a beaver's hearing is to that of a human and how well his nose compares with that of a dog.

"He probably heard you," remarked Cavit from his prone position beneath the sink. "Who could miss? I don't believe a word about how utterly silent you are in the woods."

Twelve-year-old Linda said flippantly, "A beaver could hear you a mile away, Mom."

"Then how come *you* don't hear me call you in the morning?" I asked.

"Because your first shout deafens my ears," she said, tossing her head. I was beaten.

"Never mind," soothed Nermin. "Did you really see a beaver, Mom?"

"Not quite. But I heard him splash."

Cavit's feet squirmed, and his tousled head emerged from among the pipes. "I'll tell you how to see beavers," he said. "Feed 'em."

"With what?" If I put out dog biscuits, raccoons or stray dogs might get them before the beavers did. I mentally went over a list of possible foods. Suddenly I remembered reading about a Canadian who unloaded a truckful of poplar logs where he needed a dam. Beavers found them and built his dam.

There were few poplars around our pond. But in his pasture our neighbor Pete Scavelli had hundreds which he was going to bulldoze out. I phoned Pete and asked if I could cut some.

"Take all you want," he said. "Just be sure to cut 'em close to the ground or else leave a foot or so on 'em. I don't want stubs jabbing my tractor tires."

The next weekend in Pete's field, I began thinning the dense grove of poplar saplings, with their pale green bark and swollen buds. Toward sundown I loaded a bunch of them into the station wagon and brought them to the refuge, stacking up a pile next to the barn. Some I carried deep into the woods.

Nothing stirred at the dam. I put the poplar down and left. In the morning I returned. No one was there, but to my delight the poplar was gone. A few peeled sticks floated like giant toothpicks on the water, and one long piece had been worked into the dam.

I was now reading all I could find about beavers. Through clippings mailed to me by a Canadian friend, I heard of Grey Owl, the naturalist who is credited with saving Canada's beavers from extinction. I was able to get a copy of his classic, *Pilgrims of the Wild;* and this fascinating book gave me my first inkling of the joys that beaver watching might bring.

Week after week, as I went to the dam and found the poplars gone but no beaver in sight, I became more disheartened. Could anyone but Grey Owl tame an animal as wild and wary as a beaver?

I worked my way up the creek, finding two more broken-down

dams and remnants of houses long since empty. I had read that beavers, when persecuted by man, may stop building lodges altogether and live hidden in holes in the bank. They are not naturally nocturnal or even cryptozoic (living in concealment). When the first white settlers came, beavers were moving about by day, calling to one another across the lakes. They worked on their dams in daylight and sunned themselves on top of their lodges.

That trap we had found explained a lot of things. "It's a pogrom," I muttered. "They're refugees in their own country. How can I convince them that we're their friends?"

"Keep feeding," Cavit said. "It's taken years to make them wary like this. It may take years to set things straight. Since they come out only after dark, why don't you stay there all night?" Then, seeing my hesitation, "You aren't afraid, are you? Junior'd be with you."

"I'm not afraid, exactly," I said—although I was—"but I'd be sort of . . . lonely. I couldn't take Junior. Beavers are afraid of dogs."

I did not tell Cavit that the idea of a night in the woods had already occurred to me, and I had dismissed it. I have always been afraid of the dark. Now the question was: Which was stronger, my fear of the dark or my desire to study beavers?

The following Saturday I appeared in the kitchen after dinner, carrying a flashlight and blankets. Nonchalantly I said good-bye and started for the woods.

Heavy branches closed overhead, and the full moon was blotted out by clouds. My feet knew the way, yet where a fallen pine trunk lay across the path, I stumbled, and when the blankets caught and held, I felt trapped. The way ahead was like a wall, and the blackness followed behind like padded feet. Over and over I repeated a saying I had heard: The very depth of the forest is the safest place to sleep.

It was a relief to hear the faint gurgle of water at the dam, where I had placed poplar bait earlier. Now, wrapping myself in blankets, I sat down at the base of a big pine just ten feet from the edge of the stream.

At first all was quiet except for the whisper of water running over the dam. Water and shore could just be distinguished, with black treetops towering above. As I was settling myself, an eerie call, which I recognized as the hoot of a horned owl, sounded from upstream. It moved closer, then stopped. A rustling pulse beat in the woods all around. My eyes ached from boring into the dark on all sides. When would the beaver come?

Suddenly I heard a loud snort from directly in front of me, and a swish of water told me that the sound had come from the direction of the stream. Raccoon? Otter? Could it possibly be a beaver? I waited for another snort, but there was only silence. Whatever it was must have gone away.

I stood up to stretch my legs and arms, which had become stiff in the late November night, then rearranged the blankets and curled up at the base of the pine to sleep. Almost at once I heard a skitter of mice through the fallen leaves and the dry hop of a rabbit. The soft music of the falls lulled me. I was very tired and was just about to drop off to sleep when I heard footsteps coming —a different sound from that made by mice or rabbits. Steadily the steps moved along the far edge of the creek, crackling dead grass and disturbing leaves. When a stick snapped, I sprang upright, heart pounding.

The footsteps paused. I heard a low snarl and a hiss. Then whatever it was continued on, while my mind conjured up one wild story after another. Startling and guttural, a harsh cry, like the roar of a lion, though not as loud, came from across the creek. It hung in my ears as I waited for the animal's next move. Then the cry came again from farther downstream. He had evidently departed without a sound. My admiration of his stealthy movements drove out some of my fear. But a long time passed before I dared lie down again and before I slept.

I wakened to sun in my eyes and the red squirrel scolding

madly. After limbering up, I inspected the dam and found the poplar limbs gone. Moreover, fresh mud had been pushed up, and sections of peeled poplar worked in. The beavers had eaten and worked while I lay only a few feet away. Elated, I hurried home to boast of my adventure.

Thereafter, I spent many evenings at the dam, hoping each time that a beaver would appear, but the beavers always waited until I had gone. Maddeningly, each morning revealed that they had been active during the night, cleaning up all the food, then departing for their secret daytime haunts.

That winter, we met a man who was to play a vital role in the drama of our refuge. A picture of a welder, Alfred A. Francesconi, and a story featuring his hobby of wildlife photography appeared in our local paper. One of his bird pictures had just won an award in a *Philadelphia Bulletin* contest, and he was quoted as saying: "I used to shoot with a gun. Now I use a camera. I'm going to sell my shotguns and buy more film. I'd rather have graceful pictures on the walls than meat on the table."

Cavit and I were pleased with the article. "Why not ask him over?" said Cavit. "He might find something here to snap."

So I wrote a note. A few days later the phone rang, and a strange voice spoke a name and something about a newspaper article. It was Al. He sounded a little unsure of the wisdom of calling me; I was hesitant myself, wondering what kind of a person I was inviting to the refuge.

When Al came, Junior went right up to him, tail wagging, and rested a paw on his knee. Al's wiry frame teetered on the edge of the couch, like a bird ready to take flight. In his hair was a touch of gray, but his manner was appealingly boyish. Caressing Junior's ears, Al talked about photography.

I had never owned a camera. Any pictures I made had been sketched by hand. To me a camera looked complicated and much too expensive.

"What kind of camera do you have?" Cavit asked.

"Mamiya."

We had never heard of it.

"Japanese make," he said.

"Could we see it?"

"Sure." He went out to his Ford pickup and came back carrying a gadget bag strapped over his shoulder. Slung around his neck was the cord of the Mamiya, an oblong black box. "They call me the little man with the big camera," he said.

After he had gone through all the features of the Mamiya, I was confirmed in my conviction that a camera was not for me. "Make yourself at home and get all the pictures you want," I told him. "I'll stick to sketching. How do you get through the woods with all that equipment?"

"Become a packhorse," he said, and he shouldered his pack.

As we went down the trail together, I carried my sketch pad and pencil, but I was glad someone would be taking photographs at the refuge. I told Al about the beavers.

"You tame 'em," he said. "I'll come and take their pictures."

Whiskers, Greenbrier, and Company

WINTER PASSED swiftly. I had given up part-time secretarial work, had bought an ancient typewriter, and had begun to keep meticulous records of my observations in the field. I spent every spare moment in the woods. As soon as the ice melted from the stream, I resumed putting poplar at the dam. As before, it was gone each morning. With persistence bordering on stubbornness, I continued morning and evening vigils, though Cavit had begun to tire of my obsession.

The children were bored too. "Stay home tonight, Mom," they said.

"I've become a beaver-widower," Cavit sighed, settling down to his paper after dinner. "When are you going to spend an evening with us?"

" '. . . to a different drummer,' " I retorted, but now it was almost against my will that my feet took me to the dam night after night. It was already July and I had not yet seen a beaver, although I was observing many other kinds of wildlife.

One day, near sundown, I sat waiting in full view—I could have put up a blind, but I wanted the beavers to approach me in friendship. First the wood ducks came, shaking their green crests. They mewed as they circled playfully or tipped upside down to feed on the bottom of the creek, often completely submerging. A family of wood ducklings regularly patrolled that section, and though they never ventured past me, I often saw them dabbling for insects in the water or reaching to grab a worm or moth from overhanging twigs. This time I saw the water by the old cedar snag at the bend buckle and gleam, and there were the ducklings, enjoying a new taste thrill of early blueberries. The ducklings jumped from the water, their immature wings aflutter, and snatched at the low-hanging berries, pulling them down to eat.

A muskrat paddled silently by, and a huge snapping turtle clambered up the dam and slipped into the stream above. Then came a blue heron, his long legs dangling, ready to land on the dam. But he saw me in time to retract with a start and flap wildly away. A kingfisher, rattling a challenge, streaked up the channel like a hurled dart and alighted on a cedar limb to dive after minnows.

After half an hour I saw the waters at the bend of the stream ripple in those immense waves otters make. A pair of them advanced downstream toward me, diving and feeding in a carefree manner. When they reached the fallen cedar twenty feet away, they saw me and immediately raised bristly faces for a better view. They were becoming used to my presence. One took refuge in the brushy tangle along the shore, while the other came on to reconnoiter. He snorted, approached to within ten feet, then dived, and reappeared at the far shore. The other joined him, and they sneaked through the bushes to make a wide detour around me.

As the otters departed, I heard gay singing from downstream, and a small bird came streaking like a yellow flame through the dark leaves. It was the male prothonotary warbler, who nested in an old woodpecker hole in a stub below the dam. Each evening at the same hour he came flitting up the stream, gathering his supper of insects among the leaves and often dipping into the water as he flew from one side of the creek to the other. His spirited bursts were emphasized by the languid notes of a nearby wood thrush's evening song.

It was a few evenings later, while I was again entranced by these contrasting melodies, that I saw a gray-brown bit of flotsam moving toward me down the current. I looked again and realized that a beaver—at last!—was swimming my way. She carried her head so low that only the top of her nose, her eyes, and her small ears protruded above water level. With extreme caution she hid behind the fallen cedar. I waited. There was no sound. Then a slight movement disturbed the pickerelweed at the far end of the dam; a row of silver bubbles lengthened like beads being strung swiftly on invisible thread. The beaver had stolen noiselessly over the dam and was swimming underwater down the stream. She did not come back.

As July passed into August, swamp azalea bloomed white and fresh among the cloying fragrance of sweet-pepper spikes. On the surface of the stream, pollen scum from myriad blossoms spread a gossamer roof over the creatures living below, and the sun laid wide gold and gray bars on top, like a striped awning.

I had named the beaver-feeding place Otter Dam. One evening in late August I plodded wearily there, threw down an armful of poplar sticks, and seated myself on my accustomed cedar root, taking from my pocket a book by Henry David Thoreau. For half an hour the evening chorus of birdsong formed a background to my reading. Then a hush settled over the forest, broken only by the slow, bell-like notes of the wood thrush, celebrating the end of day. It was a great pleasure to read Thoreau in a setting he would have loved. But a greater pleasure was in store.

As I sat reading in the waning light, I heard a small gurgle, and looking up, saw a broad black nose poke out from the water next to the dam, not six feet away. Up rose the head of a big beaver, her seallike whiskers all coated with pollen scum from the surface of the water. She climbed the dam four feet from me,

Whiskers in search of poplar—water willow in background

Beaver

chose a stick of leafy poplar, and settled down to eat with only the end of her flat, rounded tail in the water. I named her Whiskers.

Holding the stick in an overhand fashion, she moved it past her teeth, twirling it with slender black fingers, while her teeth worked like a lathe to take the bark off quickly and neatly. When the long stick was bare, she ran it rapidly back through her fingers, making sure that no scrap of bark was left. Then, discarding it, she selected another. To my disappointment, she swam away with it, disappearing around a clump of sweet-pepper bushes at the far shore. From out of sight came the rhythmic click-click of her teeth.

My first thought was to share this historic event with my family, who in spite of their teasing were rooting for my success. Leaving the beaver placidly gnawing, I raced home and found Linda and Nermin playing soul music in their room. I feared that with a record on the turntable my big news would not gain attention, and I was gratified to see Linda lift the needle in the middle of the piece and close the cover. The girls seemed excited and wanted to go back with me. They had shared my beaver longing more than I realized.

At the dam ten-year-old Nermin sat nearest the water, holding a twig in her hand. The beaver was not in sight, but she soon returned, swimming with head almost submerged, then raised her nose to sniff the air. She came right up to Nermin and took the twig from her hand. Moving a short distance away, she sat in shallow water to eat, while the girls changed places very quietly. Whiskers soon finished her twig and came back for more. She took a piece of poplar from Linda's hand and ate it without moving from her place at Linda's feet.

The following evening Cavit went with me to the dam, and Whiskers approached, showing very little concern at our presence—only a precautionary look and careful sniffing. It seemed that by the time she had decided to give us her confidence she was completely at ease. I would love to know what had gone on in that keen brain during the waiting period, while she checked our references.

Jubilant, I entered an intensive beaver-watching phase. I had hoped to see more, but even one beaver would do. Then one evening in September while Whiskers sat beside me eating, I saw a second beaver swimming down the stream. He hesitated for a long time under the shelter of the fallen cedar, then circled uncertainly in the pool above the dam. Finally he crossed over the dam and went on down the channel. He had seen me and not slapped his tail. That was a triumph—a sure sign that he had seen me many times before and had lost some of his wildness. I named him Greenbrier.

A few nights later he dared come for poplar, stuffing the green clusters of leaves into his mouth with relish and reaching up one hand to scratch his ear. That evening the Thoreau book again lay open on my lap as I fed Greenbrier poplar sticks with one hand. His webbed feet were almost on mine, which were booted and resting in the water. I never knew what happened just then; maybe I moved my foot. Suddenly with a "Thwack!" Greenbrier's tail hit the water, and he was gone in a swirling dive. A geyser of water leaped up, to spray in great sheets into my face, over my lap—and onto Thoreau. I am sure Thoreau would have been pleased at this baptism, but it was a pity that the water did not fall on the page where he says: "Suppose the muskrat or beaver were to turn his views to literature, what fresh views of nature would he present!"

I applauded that superb defensive gesture, the slap of a beaver's tail, while wiping my glasses and smoothing out the wet pages of the book.

Actually, my bath felt good. It had been a very dry summer, and we were involved in the worst drought in years. At the dam the roots of bushes and trees were becoming exposed as the water receded. The beavers were finding their channel narrow, which partially accounted for Greenbrier's nervousness, I learned later, since beavers are unusually cautious if their vital element gets low.

One day in the side yard by the house, I accidentally unearthed a batch of baby painted turtles, looking dry and lifeless in the arid sand. They were in the process of hatching. Two, still partly in the eggs, seemed dead. I rushed them to the house and into luke-warm water. They immediately came to life, the two in the eggs jumping out and all of them beginning to swim. I took them to the pond and let them go.

By September the paths were already carpeted with prema-turely fallen leaves and both sweet-pepper and blueberry leaves had withered on their stems. The pond had shrunk considerably, exposing wide shores of mud which had begun to dry and crack. Fearing for the beavers' water supply, we scanned the sky by day and at night listened anxiously for the patter of drops on the roof.

At last, in early October, the rains came, filling pond and stream. Muddy water grew clear again, rippling over the dam, and in quiet places, reflecting the yellow and copper of sweet-pepper, red-maple, and gum leaves and the brilliant clusters of ilex berries and chokeberries. Cedar trunks, dark with dampness, were soon thatched with thick gray lichens.

Each evening the beavers came to Otter Dam. They looked golden brown in the deep water. It always amazed me to see a beaver swimming underwater, his fists clenched close to his breast, his powerful webbed hind feet propelling him smoothly along, and his tail veering this way and that, acting as rudder and auxiliary oar.

Most times the beavers clambered onto the dam beside me, stuffing such large clumps of leaves into their mouths that they had to stop and chew with their molars awhile before swallowing. Like cows chewing their cuds, they looked thoughtful on these occasions; but unlike cows, they did not move their lips as they chewed, accentuating a meditative appearance.

I had fallen into the habit of talking to the beavers, hoping to allay their fear and accustom them to my voice. One evening Whiskers talked to *me*. She sat half in and half out of the water, peeling bark from one end of a log which she had thrust against the firm mud of the dam and eating it no-hands fashion like a Halloween party guest reaching for an apple on a string. Every few minutes she stopped to chew with her molars or to sharpen her incisors by grinding them together.

After ten minutes she sank into the water, turned, and swam straight toward me. Shielding herself behind a clump of sweet pepper which grew from a hummock in front of me, she uttered a plaintive, questioning murmur. The circumstances, and her tone and actions, led me to interpret her question: "Is it safe to come near you? You won't hurt me, will you?" Next she rounded the hummock and started nibbling lush poplar leaves at my feet. I talked to her, and she went on eating. When darkness came, I got up slowly and backed away. The contented snip-snip of her chewing followed me down the trail.

It was a long time before I heard that sound again. An early freeze closed the stream, and Otter Dam lay deserted. I did not know where the two beavers lived or how active they might be in winter.

When spring came, I once more walked along Adventure Trail, lugging poplar bait. A woodcock sprang up from the wet path and whistled away. The red squirrel, surprised at my coming, dashed up a pine trunk and from high above released a trill of chatter. I wondered if Whiskers and Greenbrier would remember me. Ice was still on the stream, and although I hardly expected to see a beaver, I did not want to be late in case they were already abroad.

Picking my way along logs which led to the dam, I was amazed to find Whiskers waiting for me. Near the fallen cedar she lay motionless in a pool of water surrounded by thin ice. As I came near, she poised her tail, ready to splash; but when I spoke, she

Whiskers, mother beaver, grooming herself

lowered it and began swimming toward me, diving under an in-
tervening spread of ice. She's gone, I thought; but soon she reappeared next to a sunken log near me. From that sheltered spot
she looked me over, then came and tugged at one of the poplars.
It was Whiskers all right, not quite so tame as last fall, but ready
to renew our friendship.

Before long we were back on our former footing. Whiskers
would come early each evening and would often climb up beside me to comb her fur or daintily nibble sticks. As she groomed
herself, using as combs her split toes—the second one on each of
her hind feet—I was able to observe her closely. Like a huge
well-stuffed teddy bear, she sat erect, bracing her plump body on
immense hind legs and broad, flexible tail. Often she sat right on
her tail, which was tucked between her legs, with the end extending in front of her. In this position she could reach handily for
the beaver's version of beauty cream, an emollient preparation
produced by glands at the base of the tail. With this rich yellowish
substance, castoreum, she meticulously and thoroughly anointed
her hair. This oil lent protection as well as beauty to Whiskers's
fur. It prevented the hair from drying out when exposed to air
and kept her from becoming waterlogged when submerged.

In performing her toilet, Whiskers parted the long reddish-
brown hairs of her outer coat to reveal the dense gray inner fur,
infinitely soft and warm, for which the beaver is famous. Like a
cat, she bit out from her fur any tangles, but there the feline
technique ended. It was with sensitive black fingertips or double-
toothed comb, and not her tongue, that she smoothed out her fur.
And unlike a cat, she scratched with front feet as well as back,
a combination which allowed her to reach any spot that itched.
Later I was to find that beavers often groom each other, one in-
itiating the rite by approaching the other with an equivalent of
our human plea: "Scratch right here, please?"

Whiskers's camaraderie was deeply satisfying to me, and as I
continued to watch her groom herself as the days went by, I

made a discovery. She was pregnant. Her blessed state was evident by increased girth, the unwonted effort with which she now hoisted herself out of the water to waddle up on the dam beside me, and finally by the enlargement of her breasts.

The big question in my mind was where the kittens would be born. All the lodges we had seen looked dilapidated and unlived-in. However, there was one clue: the beavers usually came from downstream. Their home should be somewhere along the quarter mile between the pond and Otter Dam. That was a stretch I had not yet investigated, for water spread out on either side in extensive marshland cluttered with fallen timber, matted swamp grass, and intertwined shrubs. Plunging into that quagmire required a strong incentive, which the prospect of spying on a beaver family at home now provided.

The first week in June, Whiskers did not come. I was worried, yet hopeful that she was busy with maternal chores. For three nights I put out poplar as usual without seeing hide nor hair of a beaver. My feeling of suspense grew each day, though worry was lessened by the fact that the poplar disappeared regularly during the night. Then, just as I was about to start searching for the beavers, Whiskers herself came swimming toward me at the dam, gamboling along the way. Diving with a flourish and a sidewise flip, she came up to accept a piece of poplar. Her manner suggested that surge of release experienced by a human mother who had laid away her maternity clothes and could once again look down at her knees.

My estimation of Whiskers's behavior was right. When she rose up to take poplar from my hand, I could see that she had been nursing young. A pair of long pink nipples protruded from the soft fur of her breast between her arms, and farther down was the other pair, pink and swollen with milk. With low murmurs she communicated what she could of her freedom and joy, and with my own inadequate language I tried to tell her that I understood.

Whiskers was very hungry. She pushed green leaves rapidly into

Flying squirrel on oak branch

her mouth, inserting small twigs, toothpickwise, like a housewife feeding celery into a grinder. From inside her mouth issued the rhythmic, muffled grinding of her molars, as the twigs were reduced to sawdust. She seemed uncommonly avid for greens; and when the leaves and twigs were gone, she swam away, ignoring the coarser bark, and cut herself a sweet-pepper stem, from which she nibbled only the tender leaves. Discarding the stripped stem, she sculled slowly to the dam, crept across, and swam back down the stream. To where? And when would she bring her kittens with her?

New life was everywhere that June. One day as I passed through Squirrel Haven, where an arm of the pond creeps up under tall gum trees, I surprised a mother grouse with her brood. She gave a shrill cry and flopped away, in the well-known broken-wing act. The babies had hushed their peeping and were hidden, I knew, in the leaves strewn on the forest floor. Some would be nestled under sheltering leaves, others flattened out where they stood, exposed but invisible because of their mottled browns and grays. Meanwhile, the mother tried desperately to attract my attention. She threw herself into the water crying piteously. Next she staggered out and hobbled through the underbrush, circling near me and whining like a heartbroken puppy.

Taking the hint, I walked swiftly along the path. However, I had to watch my step, for thousands of tiny toads—almost indistinguishable in color from the fallen leaves—were coming from the pond and hopping across my way.

I would make many stops on my way to Otter Dam. I usually paused to place a few peanuts at the door of the flying squirrels' home in a hollow oak. Sometimes one was waiting for me, big black eyes peering out from a furry gray and white face. He was an elfin creature, half the size of his burly cousin, the gray squirrel, who lived in a neighboring oak. He differed, of course, from the gray one in having folds of furred skin connecting his front and rear feet and in his flat, rudderlike tail, covered with short, dense fur, which allowed him to make graceful glides. I had believed these sprites to be strictly nocturnal until I often surprised them sitting at their door in the early morning or late afternoon, especially on days when the sun was overcast.

Holding out a peanut, I would step over to the oak calling softly, "Come on, come on." The snub nose would twitch like a hungry rabbit's. With pink feet gripping the edge of the hole, the little squirrel would reach out and gently take the peanut from my fingers.

Another one of my stops was at the home of Cinnamon, the raccoon. She had taken the house we put up—an outsize "bird-house" with a four-inch hole—and remodeled it to suit her taste by promptly chiseling out a back door just under a rear eave. As I walked by in the late afternoon to visit the beavers, Cinnamon would observe my passage. If she was not in sight, I would chant, "Cinnamon! Cinnamon!" Soon two round silvery ears would poke up, and a black-masked face would look out. I usually said hello and continued walking, but on one occasion I approached her home uninvited. I had seen what looked like a stick projecting six inches outside the hole. I stepped off the path to get a closer look. Standing under her house, I heard little mews and smack-ings and also got a good look at the "stick." Cinnamon, lying on her back with one hind leg stretched out the door, was nursing her young. Later she brought them to Otter Dam, where she fed near the beavers each night.

Then there was the red squirrel. I had given Old Chatterbox the name of Fiery after his blazing red tail. Later I became ac-quainted with his mate, Furry, a demure, brown-garbed matron who knew how to handle a husband. On the far side of a log at the end of the dam, I had tacked a small wooden box where I put nutmeats. Furry would always be first to meals; scurrying smartly along the mossy trail among the cedars, she would leap to the log and begin to eat. Soon Fiery would arrive, but Furry

Raccoon approaching two young beavers at dam

would not let him near the food. Turning away, he would scrabble up a nearby cedar and crouch meekly on a branch, while Furry would sit below chewing, her mouth full. It seemed she would never get through. Apparently Fiery thought so too, for he would start down the tree several times. Each time, she would yell at him and he would creep back up—for all his fiery bluster a henpecked husband.

After she had finished eating, Furry would wipe her dainty mouth on the green moss and begin to bury the leftovers among the leaves. Then she would hurry home to nurse her babies. Only then would Fiery timidly sniff for crumbs. As soon as Furry left, I would put out fresh nuts for him, so he would find more than leftovers.

The whereabouts of the beaver kittens was now the main topic of conversation in our family. Each night when he came home my husband asked, "Where are they?" The children's interest, which had waned after feeding Whiskers a few times, now perked up. They said that when I found the kits, they would have a look at them. But no one offered to help in the search, not even Al. "You find 'em," he said, "and I'll come take their pictures."

Two weeks after Whiskers had told me she was a mother there was still no sign of the kittens, and I could contain my curiosity no longer. Wearing sneakers and prepared for a dunking, I waded down the stream, in some places sinking in soft mud to my knees and in water up to my waist. Pushing aside tangled bushes and swamp grass, I stumbled on, rounding every bend with expectation. An old lodge which I thought might be the kittens' birthplace was dry and deserted. As I stood looking at it, wondering, a beaver came swimming upstream from below the lodge. It was Whiskers. She swam slowly past, giving a little murmur as I spoke to her, and continued on upstream toward Otter Dam. I looked down the way she had come. There, just before the next bend in the stream, stood a huge pile of sticks chinked with fresh, soggy mud and built around a clump of cedars. It had to be the nursery.

Turning back, I planned my campaign. I did not want to wear waders or sit soaked to the skin each time I visited the beaver kittens. So from a point directly opposite the lodge, I built a path of cedar logs from Adventure Trail out to the stream. The evening it was finished I sat on the root of a cedar just across from the lodge, abrim with curiosity and expectancy at the prospect of seeing my first baby beaver.

Under the long shadows of the setting sun, half an hour passed without a ripple in the water. Not a sound came from within the lodge. I grew restless on my cedar root, bothered by an uneasy feeling that I had no right to spy. Besides, I was not even sure that the kits were inside the lodge.

Then Whiskers came. Sensing my presence, she glanced my way, but as she showed not the slightest anxiety, my own uneasiness vanished. She tipped up and disappeared into the lodge. Almost at once there came the frenzied mewing of beaver kittens, an endearing sound—one I had never heard before but was to hear countless times thereafter. Their voices resembled the plaintive cries of hungry felines but had a quality which I was eventually to recognize as exclusive to beavers.

The cries of the kittens abated, and soon, with a swirl of water about the entrance, two baby beavers popped out. They swam awkwardly, tipping from side to side. They looked less than a foot long and had tiny paddle tails. A newborn kit may weigh only half a pound, and his fluffy fur helps keep him afloat while he learns to swim. His first swimming efforts are also aided by his mother, who may carry a young one out through the water and up to the surface while he clings to the fur on her back. She may pull him out of the water if he gets into trouble, grasping his tail gently with her teeth. But these adventurers, only a little over two weeks old, had evidently finished beginners' lessons and were on their own, as far as swimming was concerned. I could see that, like their parents, they used their hind feet and tails for swimming and kept their tiny fists bunched up against their chests.

After making a few hesitant circles, the babies went back into the lodge, finding it quite an effort to get their fluffy bodies under the water again. Then I heard mewing, which gradually subsided, and I pictured them contentedly nursing.

At this point, Greenbrier arrived and began work on his lodge, but not until he had swum nervously back and forth in front of me more than once, each time lifting his head to give me a searching look and keeping his tail poised ready to slap. That he refrained from doing so assured me that my presence near his babies was acceptable.

Greenbrier swam to a spot twenty feet below the lodge, picked up a branch ten feet long and at least five inches thick, and started towing it toward the lodge, holding the butt end of the branch in his mouth. Still swimming along, he grabbed the branch in both hands, passed it over his head, and with his teeth, got a new grip on it from the other side. This was done without once breaking his stroke, while he vigorously braced his tail to overcome the sideways drag of the load. On the way he dived to gather an armload of mud. When he reached the lodge, he rose on his hind feet, mud bundled in his arms and tucked against his chin, and stalked up the steep side, the long branch trailing from his mouth. He looked like a man struggling up the stairs with a huge bag of supplies and a long-handled broom. Dropping his load near the peak, he patted mud in place with his hands and wedged in one end of the branch. Then he quickly ambled down on all fours and slid into the water. As he continued his work, he paid no more attention to me.

Sometimes he carried up a big log, tugging and pushing strenuously until he got it to the top. I watched him for an hour or so, while the sky darkened and the moon came up. Inside, the kits were quiet; their mother was with them. Downstream a black duck began to quack. A raccoon came gliding through the reeds and peered out at me from ten feet away. After a long look he retreated without a sound, only a few reeds quivering where he had passed. Every few loads, Greenbrier knocked off for a snack, then went right back to work. When I left, he was still heaving and tugging or diving headfirst after mud with his black tail waving in the air.

A feeling of satisfaction filled me, combining the joys of discovery and anticipation. I had come, had seen, and been conquered. Leaving Greenbrier busy with his chores and Whiskers and her young at rest in the lodge, I made my way home.

After that, I went each evening to sit on the cedar root across from the lodge, sketchbook in hand, a pile of poplar twigs in the water at my feet. Though the kittens were continuously alert to danger, they played with the abandon of normal children. At any unusual noise, such as a repeated birdcall or a leaf rustling unduly, they would look up and listen, then slip into the water and circle watchfully before coming out again. Coupled with their watchfulness was an air of supreme self-confidence in their ability to cope. There was a definite swagger to their swimming, a defiance in the slap of their tails, and an unchastened bravado in the way they teased each other and their indulgent parents.

I was glad to see that the beaver kits were wary where natural dangers were concerned. While the ancient threats of wolf, wildcats, and bear were gone, a horned owl, I knew, might catch and eat a young beaver; and I often heard horned owls hoot at sunset. Sometimes I saw one fly silently by.

One sundown a horned owl came flying up the creek past me and landed on a dead stub a hundred feet away. He gazed at me stonily with his great yellow eyes. His silhouette was like that of a raccoon minus the ringed tail. After a few minutes he flew again, to alight in a dense bunch of maple growth, which hid his body but allowed his earlike tufts to protrude. Big and fierce

Male wood duck

as he was, he had his troubles too. A rowdy flock of blue jays and flickers bunched themselves around him, yelling and darting at him again and again. He stayed there for some time, then fled to new shelter. As he took off, a great cawing began, and a procession of crows came winging from the south, driving the harried owl before them.

There were many distractions to beaver watching on any given night. Directly across from my cedar-root hassock reared a stub in which the pair of prothonotary warblers had raised their young; and the mother, only a bit duller yellow than her golden mate, was engaged in feeding a baby who sat on a maple twig overhanging the stream. Each time the mother, who was perched on a limb below, reached up with food, the baby leaned so far over that he had to fan his wings to keep from falling. The feeding took place at the very time that the male was singing his rollicking song all the way up to Otter Dam. I wondered when it was father's turn to care for baby.

Wood ducks played and fed in a pool just below the lodge. While the cawing of the crows faded in the distance, I watched a young wood duck swim straight toward the spot where a big snapping turtle's head jutted up like the end of a black stick. At the same moment a muskrat swam briskly out from the brush upstream, towing a freshly cut branch of sweet pepper. (I had just heard the tiny crash of its falling.) Muskrat and duck were swiftly converging on the snapper.

When he neared the snapper, the muskrat dived smoothly, the branch he towed following him down in one limber movement. After swimming underwater between the turtle and the duck, he bobbed up and continued upstream around a bend, the green banner of pepper leaves still fluttering behind him.

The young wood duck paddled right past the snapper, who never moved. A young female glided out from the bushes, the white ellipse of her eye-patch lighting up a demure brown face. In contrast, the male's extravagant crest shone iridescent blue-green, and his bright scarlet eyes matched the red of his beak. A high snowy collar gleamed under his chin, and a chestnut-striped chest was separated from his side markings by a bold stripe of black and white. He had the air of a fiesta-bound caballero.

The two swam my way, side by side. When they saw me, they began to circle and gawk, holding their heads high and uttering little bleating calls like the weak mews of kittens. They peered out at me from under a fallen log, but they did not come near. Suddenly the female took off, uttering her characteristic cry, and the male followed silently, both blundering almost vertically up through branches, breaking off dry twigs as they rose.

A day in July brought unexpected delight. I had found that Greenbrier did not always wait until evening to get on with his maintenance work. Occasionally I surprised him at his tasks in the early morning and even at noon. He had taken to coming out regularly an hour or two before sundown, and after a brief snack, continuing work from where he had left off. Whiskers, in respite from motherly duties, sometimes came out too, leaving the babies sleeping.

This particular afternoon, Whiskers sat near me, companionably grooming her fur and talking to me from time to time with a low murmur. Greenbrier was not in sight. Giving a final pat to her fur and a scratch to her eyebrows, Whiskers ambled down the bank and eased herself into the water. Just then ripples appeared above the underwater door of the lodge, and the baby beavers popped out—one, two, three, four—and swam purposefully toward their mother. But her present mood was impatient, and she made a quick dive to avoid them. They promptly dived in around her, coming up in a roil of water and clinging to her fur. Evidently Whiskers had had a hard day, and any human mother could have identified with her vexation at the whining group. My own reaction was one of sympathy mixed with wonder at how she would solve her problem. It occurred to me that a few harsh words and a slap or two might go far. But Whiskers had other plans. Taking a long, thoughtful look my way, she turned her back on me and the kittens and swam calmly away in the direction of Otter Dam.

I expected the kittens to follow her, but they did not. Flipping their tails, circling and diving, they began to frolic in their home pool. The sun was still bright. The swamp was very green. A Maryland yellowthroat sang lightheartedly among the laurel, while downstream a family of young flickers whined and squeaked, commenting on the world outside their hole, which they were exploring that day for the very first time.

What will Greenbrier say? I wondered. Much more cautious than his mate, he might be disturbed at finding me alone with his youngsters. I did not have long to wonder. Greenbrier came plowing rapidly downstream, and seeing me there near his young ones, swam back and forth in the yellow afternoon light, his fur glinting as he dipped underwater after each mighty slap of his tail. He was disturbed indeed and indicated his wrath by the most potent means at his command. I did not know whether he was mad at me for being there or at his mate for leaving his children in such risky hands.

At the first crack of his tail, two of the youngsters dived into the lodge. The other two, playing farther away, continued to be absorbed in their game of wrestling, each trying to push the other over backward into the water. Greenbrier circled again and again, giving a vigorous slap at each turn. The two disobedient ones paid no attention. Whenever his frantic swimming brought him close to me, I spoke softly to him. Otherwise, I kept myself strictly a part of the cedar root with which I tried to blend. Inwardly, I was as upset as Greenbrier, but for a different reason. I was contributing to the worries of a devoted father, and I felt guilty. I would have slunk away, but feeling that any action on my part would only aggravate Greenbrier's alarm, I merely tried to shrink smaller and kept on muttering in a voice I hoped might reassure.

At last he came close to me and stared up intently, sniffing the air, but with his tail quiet. For a full minute, we looked each other in the eye. Then he turned, swam across the pool, dived under a log, and paddled back upstream—leaving the youngsters in my care.

Soon, out from the lodge came the two timid kittens, and all four babies clustered at my feet, stuffing their mouths full of poplar leaves. Meanwhile, the sun had set; and the moon, already high, shone through the cedars beyond the lodge, gleaming on the little circles and wavelets created by the active kittens. A bat flew overhead, uttering tiny cries. Mosquitoes hummed sharply. But I could not leave my post—I had been left in charge.

Whiskers finally returned, and her young ones hurried with eager cries to meet her. Swimming straight for the lodge, the mother tipped up and dived. The youngsters followed, leaving a glitter of bubbles in their wake. From inside the lodge came a chorus of whines and soft mewings as the babies nestled in to nurse; for in spite of momentary lapses in motherly patience, Whiskers was still suckling her kittens, who would not be weaned until two months of age. As the sounds became softer, I rose up stiffly and splashed back through the swamp toward home. The dark was sparked with fireflies and alive with singing toads. A whippoorwill called. I would have liked to stay there forever, a baby-sitter for beavers.

Each night, before settling myself at the lodge, I had been putting poplar boughs at Otter Dam. During the first two weeks after the kittens' birth, Whiskers and Greenbrier had taken turns in their forays after the poplar. Thereafter, they had left the kits untended at the lodge.

One day, when the young were about six weeks old and nearly

Whiskers and young (two months old)

weaned, one of them headed upstream after his parents. He did not come back to where his siblings were playing and I sat watching from the cedar root, alternately handing out leafy twigs and making lightning sketches of beaver poses.

I recognized those who were left as Goldie, Brownie, and Nippy. Fluffy, the boldest one, had gone. Leaving the three, I also headed for Otter Dam, where I found Whiskers and Greenbrier munching poplar bark and Fluffy, seated on the dam, holding a twig of poplar with one hand and eating it with gusto. As I sneaked near, he changed position slightly, lost his balance, and tumbled down the muddy slope of the dam and into the water with a plop. His hold on the twig never loosened, and he kept right on eating.

Thus began my role as spectator at a multiringed circus. Undecided at first about when to be where, I decided to make Otter Dam my evening post and to visit the lodge occasionally by day, when the beavers sometimes ventured out close to their home.

By this time my family had resigned themselves to my beaver haunting, but they steadfastly declined to join me. Wistful invitations were met with Linda's rebuff, "Slimy beavers! Ik!" and Nermin's, "You're going *again?*" My shoemaker's children did not want shoes. As for Ned, he was too busy with high school studies and wrestling practice to devote time or enthusiasm to beavers, though I hinted that he might get useful wrestling pointers from them. He listened dutifully as I recounted episodes but with a "Wish I could come with you, Mom," would turn to his room. Cavit, after an exhausting day of research at the lab and a forty-mile drive each way, was ready after dinner to sit down with the paper—not go out and share mosquitoes with a wife who ignored him. So I was alone most of the time. I found it hard to keep my adventures to myself.

One person, however, shared my interest and listened with increasing attention to my tales of beaver lore. Al, alert to any possibilities for photographs, had become a weekly visitor to the refuge by this time. Beavers interested him, but he could rarely get away evenings.

"You need a camera," he told me one Saturday, after listening to an account of my week with the beavers. "You have the opportunity. I don't."

"I've never taken pictures," I said. "I can't afford a camera."

"But you've got the chance of a lifetime for rare pictures. You can't afford not to get them."

"Well, I'm sketching. That'll have to do."

The following weekend Al arrived with a secondhand Graflex.

"I borrowed this from the camera shop," he said. "You can use it for a week and see how you like it." He hefted it in his hands and began explaining its features. I watched as he guided the film into the slot and deftly turned the knob. "I used to take the same care loading a gun," he said. "Now it's cameras."

"You used to love hunting," I said. "How come you gave it up?"

"I didn't give up. I'm still a hunter, and I try to be a good one. But I've switched weapons. Animals can't shoot back, and a camera's the only way to make contact. I learned with the last deer I killed. She looked up as she lay there dying, her eyes asking me, 'Why?' Taking pictures is ten times more fun, and the trophies bring a lot better memories." Snapping the camera case shut, he said, "There's your weapon," and put it in my hands.

We went outside and he showed me how to focus. "You'll make a lot of mistakes before you're an expert," he said. "And always try for the best. My motto's 'Aim at the moon, and if you miss, you might hit a star.' "

I bought the camera and produced roll after roll of low-contrast photos over which Al held a series of stern critiques. With each batch I learned something new. One weekend, handing me the latest prints, he said, "I'm going to stomp all over your camera." I felt a twinge, assuming he was tired of my second-rate work. Then my eyes fell on a night scene of two young beavers

Fluffy (three months old) being petted by author

at Otter Dam with a raccoon in the background. A wry smile
lit Al's face. "I'm going to stomp on your camera. I don't like
the competition."

My family continued good-naturedly to ridicule me about the
beavers, and Al joked about my photography. Like a baby bird
reluctant to fly, I was being pushed out of the nest; and my first
flight took me into the buoyant atmosphere of writing for publi-
cation. I had been writing stories for years and had a thick stack
of rejection slips. But now I began to put down the factual details
of my association with beavers so that I could share my experiences with others. When my first article, "My Friends the Beavers," was finished, Al put in the best of his beaver photos, and I
sent the package off to *This Week*. "If they buy it, I'll get a good
camera," I promised him and settled down to wait. Within a
month the editors took the beaver story, and I traded the old
Graflex in on a brand-new Mamiya. Meanwhile, Al was way
ahead of me with a Hasselblad and a 500-millimeter lens. At his
welding shop he worked overtime building special wildlife-pho-
tography equipment.

My yearning to spread the joys of beaver watching began to
bear fruit. Neighbors who had read the article in *This Week*
telephoned. People from other states, even Hawaii, wrote letters,
many of them expressing an interest in beavers and thanking me
for the story.

Some of the people who heard about the beavers asked permission to see them. First to come were Mrs. Helen Pease, a school-
teacher who had taught our children, and her daughter, Ruth. I
warned them that they must be very quiet or the beavers would
be frightened. Ruth promised that she would sit still, but I did
not think she could, for she was a lively eight year old. At the
dam, Ruth was given the seat of honor nearest the beavers. Her
mother sat close behind her. I stood leaning against the tall cedar.
Soon Whiskers appeared at the far end of the dam, sauntered
over, and came to our feet. She looked up at us, blinking her

eyes. I could see Ruth's hands fidget as she tried not to point. She sat hunched over, her sneakers on a log at the water's edge.

"Come on, Whiskers," I said softly. "We won't hurt you."

Reassured, the big beaver reached for a limb of poplar, and towing it across the pool, sat near a log to eat. Ruth looked up at me then, her eyes shining, but she did not say a word.

Wavy V's appeared downstream, as two beaver kittens came swimming boldly up the stream. They clambered over the dam and made a beeline for the poplar. The first was Fluffy, with Nippy close behind. I need not have worried about the young beavers being scared of strangers. They made themselves at home; Fluffy came within a few inches of Ruth's feet to choose a twig. As he sat up to eat right in front of her, Ruth could have reached out and touched him. Since on several occasions I had petted a beaver kitten on his wet, furry head, always drawing my hand back if he started to edge away, I whispered to Ruth, "Hold this twig near your knee, and if he comes to take a bite, reach down and pet him."

She was not a bit afraid, nor was her mother. My experience with other animals as well as with beavers had convinced me that they would not bite unless they felt themselves threatened in some way. I had never attempted to grab hold of one, and I knew that Ruth would not.

Ruth held out her twig and waited for Fluffy to finish what he was eating. He then waddled toward her, and reaching with his paws, grasped the end of the twig with his teeth. Ruth slowly stretched out her other hand and patted him on the head. His eyes rolled up questioningly, but he kept on eating, holding the twig with both hands and chewing the leaves. Ruth stroked the soft fur between his ears, an expression of enchantment on her face.

Again I leaned down. "Scratch behind his ears," I told her. Gently she moved her hand over and fondled that spot where a caress is welcomed by cats, dogs, horses—even beavers. Fluffy complacently continued his meal. Helen Pease looked up at me, and our eyes met in maternal empathy.

Goldie, Brownie, and Nippy were also busily eating; and once the edge was off their appetites, they started to play. Brownie and Nippy began a wrestling bout, raising their heads high above the water, clutching each other's shoulders, and shoving mightily. Grunts and whines of excitement accompanied the match. Goldie swam over beside her mother and with insistent whines began to tease. Whiskers turned away from the branch she was eating and gathered Goldie in her arms. She gave an underwater roll, surfacing with a swirl, and gently pushed Goldie away from her. That was not enough for Goldie, who promptly grasped the fur of her mother's back and climbed on her tail for a brief ride. But Whiskers had had enough. She gave a warning hiss and Goldie slid off. Looking for a new adventure, she found a bit of peeled log floating on the water and began to push it with her nose, helping it along with her hands. As the log spun around in the water and moved ahead of her, she followed, nudging it along, as a child rolls a hoop. When tired of this game, she began a series of fancy dives.

Fluffy had finished eating now and was playing a game of tag with Nippy, while Goldie and Brownie climbed back on the dam for another snack. It was time to go. As Helen, Ruth, and I stole away, Helen whispered to me, "Why, they're just like children! How can I ever wear fur again?"

Now began what we call "Beavertime" at Unexpected. More and more people found their way to the refuge, and those willing to sit still had the experience of feeding beaver kittens by hand. Children would line the shore, each holding a small branch aquiver with leaves, hoping his stick would be chosen. If it was— if a small beaver swam near, waded shoreward, then rose up on his grotesquely webbed hind feet to grasp a twig—a smile would inevitably spread over the face of the lucky child, though he dared not speak a word. Sometimes visitors would be treated to

Author with beaver kit on lap

the site of the beaver kits sitting upright like stuffed toys, gravely combing their fur with deft fingers or making an attempt to use the split claws on their hind feet. This took a lot of practice, and many times a young kit lost his balance and rolled down the bank, flipping his tail in an effort to right himself. Young or old, however, beavers never resent a dunking, having the same affinity for water that Br'er Rabbit has for the Briar Patch.

Although I welcomed visitors, I savored the many hours I spent alone, accepted by all the members of the beaver family. (Greenbrier rarely came near when guests were present.) One sunny afternoon I had a unique experience. I was seated in the middle of the dam, while the roly-poly youngsters, like animated teddy bears, ambled up and down the side of the dam and their parents ate contentedly nearby. I suddenly yearned to hold a beaver kitten in my lap.

I waited until Fluffy—ever the boldest—was gnawing bark from a two-foot stick beside me. Reaching down, I took hold of one end of the stick and began easing it toward me, then up across my knee. Fluffy, chewing away, followed the stick without hesitation, right onto my lap. He kept right on eating, while I tousled the hair on his head. His wet feet and tail soaked my clothes. It was hard to resist holding him in my hands, but respect for a wild animal's right to liberty was important to me.

Fluffy eyed me askance from time to time, but apparently he felt fairly safe. I never coaxed him to my lap again but occasionally petted him as he fed beside me. Later generations of beavers were to trust me more fully, but both Fluffy and I were pioneers, feeling our way.

Fire and Drought

DURING THE PERIOD when we were making our acquaintance with the beavers, we began to find out what hazards a wildlife refuge faced. In setting out to protect animals, we had given little thought to dangers other than man's direct interference.

It was our second spring at Unexpected, although we did not yet live there. Every weekend we worked at remodeling the cabin which would become home. Suddenly a series of the worst forest fires in twenty-five years exploded in New Jersey, as a combination of unusual dryness, high temperatures, and fast winds brought brush close to the kindling point.

One day when Cavit was out of town and the children were in school, I received a phone call from a neighbor who lived close to the refuge, which was five miles away from us.

"Looks like your woods is on fire," she said.

Driving our old station wagon, I headed for the refuge. At one place I passed a stand of pines blazing fiercely. The wind was driving the fire right toward the refuge. Smoke poured across the road ahead, and as I drove through it, black flecks of ash flew into the car and clung to my clothes. At the same time a wave of intense heat hit one side of my face. The crackle of blazing branches and the rustle of burning brush almost drowned out the distant wail of fire-engine sirens.

Two frantic deer leaped across the road ahead of me, crashing into the woods on the other side. I saw a box turtle at the edge of the road, his head raised high. I stopped the car, jumped out, and scooped him up. I had heard that turtles burrowed deep to escape forest fires, but this could not always save them. Speeding on, I watched a cottontail streak before my wheels, dodge wildly, then gain the far side of the road.

At Unexpected Road, smoky flames burned to the left. Straight ahead, in a section of forest bordering the east side of the refuge, billows of smoke rose. Farther to the east were plumes of smoke, violet and gray with touches of black, looking like some bizarre sunrise. The smoke created weird patterns, which were reflected in the beaver pond.

At our cabin the mother phoebe was brooding her eggs on the porch, and green herons were feeding in the pond. Kingbirds screamed from the treetops. The bluebird pair sat on their nesting box near the driveway.

I stood in the yard watching flames shoot up while smoke billowed and flocks of birds sped over, retreating before the fire. Looking north, I saw smoke columns from a new fire, raging through the hundreds of wooded acres butting the refuge, with only a narrow dirt road between. I learned later that deer, evidently bewildered, came into people's yards from the burning woods and allowed themselves to be petted. Families who lived in woodside homes were dressed for flight and stood out of doors while fire trucks hosed down the buildings.

Though the refuge was threatened, I faced no personal danger. Out in the broad pond stood the beaver lodge, which the fire could not touch. I could retreat there should the fire trap me. But my presence was utterly useless, and in a blind, sentimental attachment to the refuge I forgot the unnecessary risk to my car. Still, it was with reluctance that I finally left Unexpected.

I detoured where some sections of road were now blocked and drove home to wait for the children to return from school. The radio was warning people in our area to pack their belongings and be ready to flee. The school bus came early, and the children and I loaded the car. There was some difference of opinion on what was most important to take with us, but all gave top priority to the cat, the two dogs, and Ned's pair of white rats. Packing gave us something to do while the smoke rolled nearer, but it was all unnecessary. We did not have to leave home.

For a week the fires raged throughout New Jersey, and the refuge was repeatedly in danger. Our woods were unharmed, however, although at one time sparks flew within a few yards of our borders.

After the fires were out, I talked to Stanley Hughes, the division fire warden who had been in charge of control efforts by the state forest fire service in our area. "There just weren't enough men to go around," he said. "We did have one observation helicopter and one plane to drop bentonite [a clay capable of absorbing and holding water]. The day the fire broke out, though, it was too windy to fly. We did what we could from the ground. One time we were on duty for a seventy-two-hour stretch. In the field men worked till they dropped. The women tried to get to them with sandwiches and coffee."

I asked Hughes why such disastrous fires should occur in the spring.

"Several reasons," he said. "For one thing, our forests are mostly oaks, maples, and other deciduous trees. They drop their leaves in the fall. The dead leaves cure and dry on the forest floor. In the spring, the sun shines directly on this dry duff through leafless trees. A carelessly tossed match, a spark from burning trash, or a smoldering cigarette butt flares up instead of going out. Once the leaves come out in mid-May, and we have a good soaking rain, the forest floor is shaded and keeps its moisture.

"With conifers it's different. They drop dry needles, and these are dried out more by summer winds. A prolonged drought makes evergreen forests tinder, and summer fires are bad. They get into the turf and are hard to put out. But our worst fire potential is in the spring."

Hughes was concerned about the wild animals who suffer from forest fires. Most birds escape early spring fires, he said, since their nestings occur after the forests have leafed out. But this is not the case with early-nesting ducks; owls, hawks, or squirrels with young in home trees; or slow-moving opossums.

Forest-fire fighters often turn aside to try and save endangered animals, he recounted. One fire fighter rescued two partly burned rabbits, stashing them in the cab of his truck. Another warden watched helplessly as two rabbits dashed past him, their fur ablaze. One saw a rabbit swim a stream to safety.

The forest fire service makes a steady effort to keep the public aware of fire hazards. "We show Smokey the Bear movies to children, movies of actual fires to adults," Hughes said. "People gradually learn. But each person who moves out from the city to the country creates new danger. He's not oriented and doesn't realize how easily a little trash fire can spread. We have to sell the idea of the value of forests—and how vulnerable they are."

He explained the fire-permit system, whereby a person getting a permit to burn is told the rules, cautioned about the danger, and warned that he is legally responsible for any fire he starts, no matter how accidental it may be.

"What should you do if you see a forest fire?" I asked.

"Simply go to the nearest phone and call the operator. Say, 'I want to report a forest fire.' Hold onto the line till she connects you with the fire warden, then tell him where the fire is and give him any other information he may ask for."

This information settled into my mind—and lay dormant until I had occasion to use it five years later.

The summer after the fires hardly a drop of rain fell. In August Cavit and I grew anxious as we saw water receding from the shores of our pond. The little cove in front of the house lay empty, baking in a hot sun; and instead of looking out from our windows on an expanse of sparkling water, we gazed on an unnatural waste of mud alternating with stagnant pools.

Up at Otter Dam, our beaver family, who still came for the poplar we provided, crawled through mud along a drying creek bed, robbed of both comfort and safety. One evening they failed to come. The poplar boughs were untouched. Hastening to the lodge, I saw that the entrance now lay exposed above the waterline. The beavers had gone.

The next night I stationed myself at the dam, but again no beavers appeared. Just at dusk, Fiery, the red squirrel, arrived to take a drink. Chittering nervously, he flicked his tail and advanced by stages along the fallen cedar, which now stretched high above a puddle of stale water. Leaping lightly to a low branch, he leaned over to drink, a sip at a time with a cautious look around between sips, and then he hurried back to the pine tops. Later a deer stepped warily out from the far shore and advanced with mincing steps through the mud. Reaching the pool, she lowered her head to drink. Just then, aware of me, she whirled and with a mighty bound crashed back into the woods.

Greatly disturbed by the beavers' absence, I pushed three or four miles up the stream bed, past pools of stagnant water bordered with mud, looking for them. Broken dams, remnants of old food rafts, and crumbling lodges showed there had been no beavers along that section for years. The situation looked bad to me, and disheartened, I turned homeward. Where were Whiskers, Greenbrier, and their family? Had they left us to look for water? And where would they find it?

I continued to search, finally venturing down below the dam of the main pond into a timbered morass I had never entered before. I found a comparative abundance of water flooding the bases of maple and cedar and standing high on the stems of

Great blue heron

sweet-pepper and blueberry bushes. I was amazed to find no sign of drought. Here were coolness, refreshing shade, and plenty of water. Soon I found the reason. Fresh mud was plastered on an old beaver lodge, whose entrances were out of sight under deep water. Just below the lodge was a newly repaired dam, which had created this reservoir. Though I did not see the beavers, I knew they were there.

That evening, I spread poplar boughs along the shore below this dam and sat down to wait, keeping my eyes on the lodge. Shadows grew long as the sun sank beyond the woods at the head of the pond. A great blue heron flapped slowly overhead, set his long wings, and glided down an aerial path through the treetops to settle on the beavers' lodge. He stood erect and uttered a hoarse "Quawk!" before crouching to stalk down the side of the lodge and step into the stream. I watched his slim-jim figure hunch along and envied him, for the beavers and other wildlife trusted him more than they did me.

Just as dusk began to dim the scene before me, water moved at the side of the lodge, and a small brown head popped up. A young beaver came swimming up the stream toward me, and I recognized Goldie, the blond one, who after Fluffy was the boldest of the four. She swam near the poplar, sniffed, and circled, seemingly undecided. When I held out a branch to her, she backed away. Then she dived, and bubbles on the water's surface followed her progress down to the lodge. Evidently the stress of relocation had made her more timid than before.

I anticipated trouble in reestablishing friendly relations, but after a few days the whole family emerged from their new home just before sunset to partake of the bountiful poplar. Gladly I took up beaver watching again.

The stream level above the pond steadily sank, until what little water remained lay in widely separated pools. I wondered how long the beavers' last-ditch supply could last. Taking my clippers, I began making a narrow trail through the wilderness below the main dam, heading along the creek toward a bridge which crossed Unexpected Road, nearly a mile to the northeast. There were so many holes in the ground that, in trying to avoid sinking into them, it took me almost a week to hack my way through the tangled brush. Some of these holes were around stumps left when fallen trunks had rotted away; others were gaps in the bog covered over by vegetation; still others were old plunge holes created by beavers for quick access to the safety of water.

As I made my way downstream, I was surprised at every turn by the plenitude of water. At intervals of about a hundred feet, small new dams cut the creek, and each held back its share of water in a generous pool. Along the banks on each side gleamed new-cut stumps. Piles of white chips showed the teeth marks of Greenbrier and his clan; wet mud glistened; mossy logs showed green. And one day Fluffy appeared in a deep pool, swimming along the bank near me. He circled briskly, regarding me with interest.

"Hi!" I called. "You're doing a great job." He gave me an arrogant look, flipped his tail, and was gone.

I felt I could leave the stream to the beavers' care.

All of New Jersey and Pennsylvania, and even New York City, were threatened with a critical water shortage that summer. Various means to beat the drought, to the tune of many thousands of dollars, were being discussed. Lost amid these grandiose schemes was a suggestion that appeared in a tiny article in the *Philadelphia Inquirer*, based on an interview with R. W. Howard, a lumberman of Emporium, Pennsylvania. Howard had written a letter to the mayor of Philadelphia, telling how beavers could help in the drought situation. He suggested the release of 100 pairs of beavers in the upper reaches of the Delaware River valley. Through the dams the beavers would build, he said, enough water would be stored to permeate the ground, raise the water table, and fill the springs, which had now gone dry. He pointed out additional long-range benefits, such as excellent fishing sites and the tourist attraction of beaver colonies.

Nothing came of his suggestions. The planners were too busy impressing the public with million-dollar programs.

Cavit and I, having seen firsthand—albeit on a small scale—what beavers accomplished as water conservators, wrote letters ourselves to local authorities and to newspapers, but without result. Howard had more confidence and more persistence than we. Aware that many parts of the country are periodically menaced by spring floods followed by severe drought, he wrote to President Lyndon Johnson recommending the purchase of 10,000 pairs of mated beavers from Canada (where some claim that beavers are too numerous) to be released, a few pairs to a locality, all over the United States. He asked that a federal law be established to protect them.

I wrote to Howard for more information. In his answer, he recounted the beaver history of his own community in northwest Pennsylvania. In his youth, it was an offense to destroy beaver dams. At least several dams were to be found on every stream.

In 1914 a pair of beavers was released. Three years later, he said, another pair was released; and from this small beginning, in sixteen years their number grew to several thousands. Today, however, hunters have eliminated all but a few colonies.

Howard felt that areas in the eastern United States, especially around Philadelphia and New York, were suffering now because man did not appreciate the beavers' worth. The members of various game commissions, whose job was to protect wildlife, destroyed beaver colonies and their dams and consequently the water supply the beavers had created. This water supply had provided spawning grounds for trout, bass, and other fish, a valuable asset overlooked by the game commissions. Howard stated that perhaps it was now the time for the legislatures of the four Delaware states to recognize the beavers' contribution and act to protect them.

Though beavers are only a partial factor in drought control, I joined Howard in the hope that his words would be heeded. His letters were written at a time when the governor of Pennsylvania had just declared forty-seven of sixty-seven counties disaster areas because of drought, and New Jersey and New York City authorities were desperate for an answer to the drought problem. Howard's words were serious, and they offered a concrete, long-term, ecologically sound solution for at least part of the problem. But they were treated in a flippant manner by the press and ignored by the powers that were. My letters too were ignored. A humble remedy is often scorned by those intent on prestige or interested in spending huge sums of money.

In September we had two small showers, which barely wet the barren earth, and the water was quickly absorbed by dry mud in the pond. October brought a downpour accompanied by a high wind. In the first hour of this deluge, paths in the woods were carpeted with tan leaves of sassafras, and the red confetti of sour-gum leaves was swept into windrows by the surging water. But the rain did not last out the night. Before morning the moon was shining out of a clear sky.

The thirsty ground soaked up every drop of moisture, so the water level in the stream was little changed. Before the rain, low water had again exposed the entrances to the occupied beaver lodge, and the beavers had once more disappeared. They came no more to eat poplar, and I did not see them again that fall. Not knowing all their habits, I assumed that they were sound asleep for the winter, perhaps in some hole in the bank.

During November we had normal soaking rainfalls. The stream was replenished and the pond itself finally overflowed. It was good to look out over water again, to see our tiny cove filled to the brim, and to hear the gurgle of the main dam, which was only 400 feet from our door.

The winter was a busy one for me. With three children going

Vole (short-tailed mouse) who inhabits beaver lodge

to school there was plenty of work inside the house, and I was trying to write. At the same time, my interest in photography increased. Since the beavers had gone, Al suggested that I take photographs of a drumming grouse that I had watched for two springs as I sat hidden behind a clump of laurel not far from Otter Dam. We set up a burlap blind ten feet from the grouse's customary drumming log.

By February grouse were already dancing in open spaces among the trees, and by late March their peak drumming season was approaching. At 5:30 one morning, I entered the blind and set up the camera. Heavy fog enfolded the woods as the sun rose. Mallards called from the distant pond, and the whistling of wings in the mist told of ducks flying to their day's adventures. Quail began to whistle, then cardinals, titmice, chickadees. A vole ran out of his hole and scampered among the leaves. Shivering, I watched first the vole, then a gray squirrel, and finally a red squirrel use the worn log as a runway. There was no sign of the grouse. Two hours later I straightened cramped legs and crept from the blind, my first attempt a failure.

Since I took the children to the bus stop each school day, I could spend only two mornings a week at the blind. Rain spoiled some chances, and a couple of times I frightened the grouse away when I came. It was not until late April that I had an opportunity to see him perform. Determined to be in time, I had arisen at 3:30 A.M. and made my way to the blind, entering it, I hoped, undetected. Only a few minutes later I heard a muffled wingbeat, and there was the grouse, drumming just ten feet away in the darkness. By the time he drummed a second time I could just make out the flurry of his wings. At that moment it began to rain. The light drizzle did not bother the grouse; but it made my camera useless, for the lens extended beyond the roof of the blind. Gradually the shape of the grouse took form, until I could see first his dark ruff and then his head and the markings on his breast. In the misty light he appeared pale gray, with deep gray markings arranged in differing patterns all over his body. His slender chickenlike feet and legs were silvery gray.

Several days later, in the blind at 4:30 with the camera ready, I again waited for the grouse to come. Soon I heard a thump in front of me, and he was there on the log. I could not see him, but his wings beat the air audibly several times, faster and faster, ending with a climactic, rustling whir. After perhaps ten minutes he drummed again. It was another half hour, however, before I could focus on his slim gray toes, which showed clearly against the green moss. The feathers on his breast were still indistinct when he walked off the log and began to stroll, picking insects from the leafy floor and pausing to nip buds from lower branches.

The sun had risen now and the air was warm. I was afraid that the grouse's morning stint was over, but he once again hopped onto the end of the log and strutted halfway along its length to his accustomed spot. His feathers had appeared gray before, but now I saw that they were buff, with russet touches and black-and-white stripes and with a coppery bib, which gleamed under his throat. Between bouts of drumming he preened his plumage, occasionally reaching back to groom his tail, feather by feather, which he raised higher than his head to show off the black-and-white bars that offset the tan. He was a rufous-phase grouse; that is, a reddish-brown type with a brilliant fox-red tail.

Again and again I snapped his portrait. Nothing I did with the camera seemed to bother him. And, happily, my first grouse pictures were a success.

During March and April I had looked halfheartedly for the beavers. Although rain had filled all their old haunts, there was no sign of life at any of the lodges. My fear was that the drought had forced them to travel down the stream and far beyond the refuge in a search for adequate water. But I should have known Greenbrier better. One day, exploring unfrequented territory at the head of the pond, I saw wet mud, evidently fresh, on an old lodge which had been bolstered with crossed sticks. Greenbrier

Grouse drumming

had returned to try the old territory. This lodge was between the babies' birthplace and the pond, in a place where the best water supply would be available.

His new location held small aesthetic appeal. Instead of water willow bending to the current, fragrant sweet-pepper bushes, and wind whispering in tall treetops, here stretched sparse swamp grass, with jagged stubs jutting everywhere like broken arrows sticking into the watery mud. But Greenbrier, choosing from necessity, had selected well. The lodge was right on the channel at the place where it joined the spreading waters of the pond. He would soon have an intricate system of underwater roads in operation, leading to the shores and honeycombing the marsh.

Evenings, I hurried to the lodge to renew acquaintance with the beavers. There was no path, so I sloshed out in three-quarter boots and did my beaver watching from a board seat, whose pointed legs were thrust into the underwater mud. Like Greenbrier, I was forced to adapt to changed conditions. My husband, meanwhile, sat at home with his paper and engineering reports, resigned to the will of Allah, who had made him a beaver-widower. He still insisted that his work left him too tired to rush into the wilds at the end of the day.

The bleakness of the beavers' surroundings was enlivened by a bluebird pair nesting in one of the stubs nearby and a downy-woodpecker family in a dead cedar close against the lodge. From this lodge each evening, Greenbrier and Whiskers swam a quarter mile to our cove to eat poplar boughs. No other beavers appeared. Whiskers was pregnant again, however, and I looked forward to meeting the young.

Leaves had appeared on the swamp maples, when one evening early in May, Greenbrier came alone to the poplar at the cove, where I was watching. He circled and sniffed before entering the cove, then approached the branches with utmost caution. He always seemed more wary when Whiskers was not with him. Taking hold of a branch entangled with others, he towed the whole bunch away, making for the head of the pond. He swam with his head on one side, his body twisted, and his tail worked hard to overcome the yaw of the extravagant load he carried. I ran along the bank and through the swamp, and outdistancing Greenbrier, waded to the lodge. All was silent there.

Soon Greenbrier appeared, and he dived into the lodge, dragging his gift of branches in after him. From within the lodge came low voices of greeting, and then the rhythmic sound of gnawing on bark. Whiskers was having breakfast in bed! This was a good sign that she had newborn kits, although I could hear no infant voices. The next night Greenbrier again came alone to the cove and hustled off to the lodge with an offering.

Four nights later, when I flashed a light into the cove, there sat Whiskers, eating calmly in the dusk. "Hi, Whiskers!" I called. "How are the babies?" She did not speak but kept on eating in the light of the flash, which I kept from shining directly into her eyes. Then she dived. Trying to pick her up with the beam, I found her swimming right toward me, her body golden brown under the water, her front feet tucked up onto her breast. She surfaced and passed close to me, giving a murmured greeting, as she went to select a poplar stick from the pile. She took it across the cove and sat in shallow water to eat.

I raced up to the lodge to see what was going on in her absence. Had she left such young babies alone? I was almost there when my rapid pace through the water caused me to stumble and fall headlong with a prodigious splash. Greenbrier appeared at once and lay watchfully for a moment on the surface. Then he gave a smart slap and dived. Coming to the surface, he started the fast circling that presaged another "Whack!" I spoke to him, trying to allay his fears. After two minutes of swimming back and forth uncertainly, he slipped back into the lodge. Just then I heard little mews; the kittens were there.

My clothing was drenched, but I had managed to hold my camera above water. I continued to wade out to the board next to the lodge and had not sat there long before Whiskers returned. Carrying in her mouth a few twigs with tender leaves, she dived into the lodge. Her voice and Greenbrier's mingled in greeting, and the kittens heightened their cries.

Soon Greenbrier emerged, lay studying me carefully, then swam over to some dead cedars standing in the water and stripped off a mouthful of bark. This he carried back inside his home.

About that time I began to be very conscious of my clammy clothes, and I decided to call it a night. And a successful night it had been, in spite of my mishap. I had found out that the father of newborn beaver kittens stays on guard while the mother is away. And I discovered also that even when Greenbrier's protective feelings were at their strongest, he had confidence enough in me to give me his trust.

By mid-May, swamp grasses were spearing the surface of the water. Water-lily rafts had not yet appeared, but the beavers fed on their succulent underwater shoots. Early blueberries dropped blossoms into the water, and swamp maples pushed out scarlet keys among their leaves. By the time the first mosquitoes appeared, the pond had come alive with the thrum of bullfrogs, the trill of toads, and the click of cricket frogs. I often heard the beaver kittens mewing and sometimes the sound of Whiskers's teeth. She was shredding poplar sticks and cedar bark stripped from standing trees, which Greenbrier helped her collect for bedding. Like squirrels and some other animals, beavers seem to know that cedar discourages parasitic insects.

There was much mystery about the lodge those late spring days. From inside came muffled splashes and infant murmurs. Long hisses indicated disagreement, and the soft plop of bodies told of youngsters playing in their indoor pool.

Before the end of May the newcomers came out of the lodge for the first time. Both parents swam together to the cove now, leaving the young at home, where I saw them frolicking just before dark, taking adventurous little swims, and feeding on lilies and twigs. I never saw more than two at a time, so I did not know how many there were. Although Greenbrier and Whiskers were as tame as ever, they did not bring the kits to the cove; and these young ones, unlike the former brood, stayed close by the lodge where the deep water afforded me no opportunity to feed them. This time the beavers were growing up without me.

Again that summer we were faced with drought. We had had no rain since April, and by early July the stream above the pond had shrunk to nothing. The water level at the lodge sank daily until mud glistened all around. The entrances were half-exposed, and the beavers had moved out. Where to?

Stumps appeared all over the shrunken pond, and the cove was connected to the main body by a mere thread of water. Each night Greenbrier and Whiskers waded in to eat, but they waited now until after dark. Noting their hesitancy, I took poplars out to the dam where the water was deeper, and the beavers then began to come earlier. The kittens did not show up at all, and I had no idea where they were staying.

Then one moonlit July night, two baby beavers appeared with their mother and father. Greenbrier grabbed a leafy branch and towed it up the channel toward the big lodge in the center of the pond—the deserted lodge where we had long ago found the unsprung trap. A few nights later I saw several beavers come streaming down the channel at dusk and realized that the whole family was sheltered there.

Late July was cool with brilliant sunsets—but still no rain. Each day I watched Greenbrier, Whiskers, and the two babies as they came from the lodge, often while the sun still shone. One evening, after Whiskers and two babies had arrived, Greenbrier came with three more! All five began nibbling leaves alongside their parents, who sat placidly eating. Then one kitten came up the bank and let me pet him while he took a twig from my hand. I called him Fluffy the Second, for he was a bold prankster ready to climb on my knee and slyly grab a bit of poplar, then scoot away with a defiant dive, splashing my legs. The other kittens too were evidently influenced by their parents' confidence, for they came freely and let me feed and pet them from the first.

As the water level continued to drop, water lilies blossomed unnaturally, their flowers being held high above the water instead of floating on the surface. Patches of bare mud grew wider, stumps multiplied, and dead trees showed rings two feet above the waterline. Much of the mud was drying and cracking into a pattern like crazed pottery. Wads of lily pads lay rotting in the sun.

Across the pond scurried companies of killdeers and spotted sandpipers. Flocks of red-winged blackbirds and starlings descended on the dying lilies to turn over the leaves and pick insects from the undersides. Water had long since ceased pouring over the main dam, and the stream bed was dry for miles above it. What water remained in our pond lay in smelly pools along the channel, where fish lay gasping—sunfish turning over on their sides, the more hardy catfish crowding the surface, gulping air.

Crows visited the pond in little groups and found plenty of carrion to feed upon. Green herons too reaped a harvest, and at sundown great blue herons would drop down to feed. The pond became a broad cuneiform tablet with bird-track hieroglyphics baked in by the sun. In the bordering woods, sweet-pepper and blueberry bushes had turned brown, and some of the trees were prematurely losing their leaves.

Cavit, rather indifferent to the beavers when all was going well, was now deeply concerned. He had identified himself with Greenbrier, and he began to put his engineer's mind to work on the big beaver's problem. Linda and Nermin undertook to save the fish, who were the most obvious sufferers. Daily the girls spent hours scooping up the stranded fish into buckets of water and pouring them into the dwindling main channel although the water there was already crowded.

The hot days went by slowly. Wherever the mud had dried out, marsh grass now sprang up from dormant seeds, making portions of the pond resemble a newly seeded hayfield. Then, as the mud baked further, the green withered away. Each day the channel water became more murky and more fish lay dead.

When we saw the beavers plodding through soft mud along a waterless stream bed below the dam, we decided something had to be done. But every idea that occurred to us required money, of which we had little. We abandoned one scheme after another. The next time we saw Al, we asked his advice. He too had been thinking about the plight of the beavers. "I've got a pump," he said. "Used to hook up sprinklers for my lawn. It might do some good."

"Great! We can put a deep well in at the pond head," said Cavit. "Pump the water and let it flow into the pond. It would rescue the lodge there and continue on down the channel. I'll go in hock for the well.".

While Al drove home to get the pump, Cavit started calling well drillers. To his chagrin he found that drilling outfits were working overtime trying to keep up with the demand. House wells were going dry; irrigation ditches stood empty. "Can't do it," the men said. "Sorry."

Al came back with his pump. The one source of water was our house well, but it was only fifty feet deep, and we expected it to run dry any minute. I was sure Cavit would never tap that. I was mistaken. He set his jaw and said, "We'll hook the pump to the well we have. Maybe we can keep a trickle going until we get a deep well—or it rains." All three of us looked up at the brassy sky, where a bright August sun blazed. Then the men got busy on the pump.

By mid-afternoon the rusty Gould pyramid pump was wired to our generator, and we had placed old rain gutters across the driveway, leading down into the cove. Everything was ready. Cavit touched the switch to set the water flowing. It gushed, cold and lovely, out of the mouth of the pump and ran down the rain spouts to fall on the mud of the dried-up cove. Gleefully we watched the dark patch spread over the gray. We then dug a ditch to connect with the main pond, hoping the water would find its way out to the channel, 400 feet away.

We soon realized our plan was not going to work. When the water hit the vast mud of the pond it vanished, absorbed by a gigantic thirty-acre blotter. But we ran the pump until 10:00 and at 5:30 the next morning turned it on again, determined to keep trying. (Ironically, at that moment torrential rains were causing flash floods in northern New Jersey, but no drop of rain came near us.)

While the old pump pounded away and the generator labored, I went for a walk below the dam, passing the previous year's lodge with its exposed entrances and forcing my way through waist-high water willow and saw grass. The sharp-toothed grass interlaced itself around my legs, meshing like a closed zipper. I had not been down there for a long time. Occupied at the new lodge and then busy with other things, I had failed to revisit Greenbrier's series of small dams all along the way. Now, coming from the parched yard and blistered mud, it was a relief to find myself in the world of the beavers, however precarious it was at the moment. Huge trees met overhead in perpetual shade. Even with little water, cool moss remained along the narrow stream bed, and the mud was still wet.

The dams, though, were lifeless. There was no current flowing in the low water standing on each side of them. I had progressed 500 feet below the lodge when I noticed higher water ahead. On the shore, the earth was flattened and swept by frequent use. I saw otter droppings and then suddenly heard a familiar coughing bark from the other side. There stood an otter, head up, barking at me. I had heard the same bark at Otter Dam. So this was where the otters hung out. I had often wondered, when I watched them travel up and down the stream.

Stopping, I spoke to the otter, and he barked at me again. For five minutes we stood conversing, and then I slowly walked on, looking back until I rounded the next bend. The otter remained barking on the bank, now and then making a feint as if to come after me. I was jubilant. Perhaps I had discovered an otter home. What else would cause him to stand his ground like that? Before, whenever I had met otters, they had snorted, maneuvered suspiciously, then glided away.

Going on down the stream, I was astonished to find the water getting deeper, though it was still far below the tops of the dams. Increasingly the water looked roiled. When I found a stump recently cut by beaver teeth, I wondered if Fluffy the First, over a year old now, could be living alone down here. Was he the sole survivor of last year's offspring or the only one who had not left for new grounds? Around every curve I expected to find a lodge. But as I kept on, I saw nothing but muddy water, floating bitten-off water plants, and at one point, a big cedar root which had been taken from the creek bottom and hauled onto the bank.

More and more mystified, I neared the end of the dense woods, where cedars were replaced by swamp maples; here, the woods gave way to a marsh, which reached to Unexpected Road. There among the last of the cedars, I found the cause of the high water. Stretched across the stream at a neck where both banks were high, and curved in a perfect arc, was a freshly made beaver dam, formed of crooked roots of cedar and well plastered with black mud. Above the dam, water stood three feet deep, and below it trickled a tiny current, seeping through loose sticks at the top. I followed the stream, which was small but flowing—the first moving water I had seen in weeks.

When I retraced my steps homeward, it was with new respect for Greenbrier. He had picked a spot well below a still-active spring, at a place where water could deepen without overflowing to the sides. But he had not been able to save his lodge; he and his family, I later learned, were living in holes in the bank.

It was not long before we realized that water from the well was not reaching the fish. Other steps would have to be taken. Al and Cavit hit on the idea of using irrigation pipe to carry the water over the dike to the channel. But they found that every inch of available pipe was in use for crops. Then Cavit suggested fire hose. We were able to get six local fire companies to lend a section or more each. The end of the combined sections of hose reached just over the dam to the drying pool below, where Cavit propped it on crossed sticks. "Turn on the water," he shouted. Al flipped the switch; and the hose, writhing and twisting like a snake, bellied out as the water pushed its way through. Below the dam Cavit waited, then gave a yell as the stream of water gushed out the end of the hose. The pump's engine roared and the flywheel whirred. "We don't mess around," said Al.

Late in the afternoon Cavit and I went to the dam and sat down to see what the beavers would do. The sparkling water invested the muddy water with fresh life. On the bank lay a pile of succulent poplar. Whiskers waded laboriously up the channel, hauling herself over logs and sinking deep in mud. She circled the pool warily; then, as Cavit called, "Come on, Whiskers, how about a drink?" she came waddling right up to the end of the hose. Thrusting her muzzle into the water's flow, she took a long cool drink.

Not until a month later did the rain come, and then it kept on for days. Puddles and lakes lay everywhere in the fields, and ruts in our dirt road were running full. All the way out to our mailbox, water moved along the sandy tracks in narrow ripples, like the backbones of snakes. Each time a lull came, the water drained off or soaked into the ground. When the sun finally shone again, it was with relief that we dismantled the pump and engine and dried out the fire hose. The beavers were safe.

Already Greenbrier had taken steps to insure a better water supply in the future. A few hundred feet beyond his first masterpiece, he had constructed another dam; then farther down, still another. Rain had filled each broad basin to the brim.

Getting to Know Otters

THOUGH WE CONSIDERED the drought a disaster, it was only when water deserted all but the deepest channels, and fish were concentrated in a few scant pools, that the otters came near, and we got to know them.

Otter Dam was so called not solely because of the otters who passed there so often. Each year close beside this dam, otters scraped up their "mud pies," which resemble beaver markers but have far less mud. Those we found were mostly heaps of duff and pine needles scratched into rough cones and topped with fishy droppings or a thick greenish substance. Each pile, we knew, held a message for any fellow otters who might come along.

Long before the first drought I had heard or seen otters passing, as they sometimes traveled by day, perhaps ranging along fifty miles of stream and going regular rounds. One fall day I saw an otter family playing and feeding in a pool below the dike. Junior was loping ahead of me, and before I could whisper sternly, "Stay back!" he and the mother otter had sighted each other. She gave a warning snort, then glided directly in front of Junior onto the dike, only four feet away.

I had my first good look at a wild otter out of water. She was average in size: about twenty-five pounds in weight and about four feet long, with a one-foot, rounded tail tapering to a blunt point. Her short legs and low-hung belly gave her somewhat the appearance of a sleek dachshund. With her wet fur, blunt be-whiskered snout, and small rounded ears, she looked very much like a streamlined beaver. Her long neck, sinuous manner, and slender tail were what distinguished her, however.

I could see that the young, alert and vigorous, were about half the size of their mother. Although they had been born in the spring, possibly as early as January, they were still dependent on their mother. This was evident by her solicitude.

I watched the anxious mother slip into the pond and reappear twenty feet out near a group of dead trees. From this point, par-tially camouflaged, she advised her youngsters with snorts and snuffles. The young churned about indecisively, answering their mother with puppylike yips. After a minute, they sneaked out of the water and wriggled out of sight among the bushes down-stream. Apparently their mother had sent them away. I turned back, sending Junior on ahead of me. After walking about a hun-dred feet, I looked around—just in time to see the mother otter's tail vanish over the dike on her way to rejoin her young.

Occasionally I had glimpsed an otter near my boat, and once a whole family had porpoised gayly through the cove. One winter I had seen a pair gallop across the frozen, snow-covered surface of the pond, alternating their frisky bounds with long slides in the snow. I read everything I could find about otters—about their long travels, their close-knit family life, their effervescent good spirits, and their enthusiasm for play.

I also learned that the otter has been decimated down through the years. The early settlers were the first to rate the fur of the otter the highest of all animal pelts in terms of durability (the beaver's fur was rated next). In addition to his desire for the otter's matchless fur, man trapped the animals in the belief, still held today, that they catch and eat fish, thus depleting trout streams. In Wisconsin, for instance, the game division made a recommendation for an open otter season, even though wilderness adventurers were traversing thousands of miles of waterways without seeing an otter. Carl Marty, noted Wisconsin woodsman and humanitarian, who through his own efforts was instrumental in getting 25,000 acres of land closed to hunting, blamed this dearth of otters on the practice of allowing trapping in the nursing season, a practice which went on with the approval of his state conservation commission. Fee-hungry wildlife managers in other states (including New Jersey) were yielding to the demands of trappers and the complaints of misinformed fishermen and were establishing open seasons. At the same time, research in other countries where the otter is protected, was proving that the otter actually aids the fish population by preying on the sick and slow. In addition, he eats turtles, crayfish, and snakes, which in turn prey on fish eggs.

Though my knowledge was limited, I agreed with Marty and scores of other preservationists who reasoned that, since otters and fish have lived side by side for centuries, the otter is no threat to a balanced fish population.

Among the otter lore I had read was Ernest Thompson Seton's tribute, "The Soul of the Otter," which most deeply impressed me:

> Of all the beasts whose Lives I have tried to tell, there is one that stands forth, the Chevalier Bayard of the wilds— without fear and without reproach. That is the Otter, the joyful, keen, and fearless Otter; mild and loving to his own kind, and gentle with his neighbor of the stream; full of play and gladness in his life, full of courage in his stress; ideal in his home, steadfast in death; the noblest little soul that ever went four-footed through the woods.

Otters, of course, were not likely to replace beavers in my affections, but I was willing to concede them second place. There was one flaw, however, in our potential relationship. Otters were reputed by many to be the enemies of beavers. It was with mixed feelings, therefore, that I pondered Seton's statement about "the noblest little soul." Cavit, by this time devoted to the beaver family, was ready to kill the otters should they threaten the beavers' safety. I had accepted the horned owl as part of nature's scheme, but could I stand by while the swift otters pursued the beavers into their home and devoured them? It was with whetted curiosity tempered by these misgivings that I continued my observations of otters.

At 7:30 in the morning on the first day of August, Cavit had gone to work and I was washing dishes. Through the window I saw several gray forms ooze up over the dike and sink into the main pond. I rushed out the door, crept along the dike to the dam, and lay in wait beside a tangle of greenbriers. The otters were a hundred feet up the channel by then, capturing fish and sometimes taking them up on the dry mud banks to eat. They were headed up the channel away from me, but for half an hour I watched them as they dived and surfaced, chased each other playfully, or sat on the banks eating. The morning sun sparkled on their wet gray heads. Tufts of glistening whiskers almost veiled their faces. Buff patches showed on their throats, but the rest of their fur, actually a rich, glossy brown, appeared dark gray only when wet.

I could tell by their sizes that the group was made up of parents and two cubs. The latter—who could have swum circles around a beaver—twisted, turned, lunged, and dived with seallike, liquid grace. Watching them, it was hard for me to realize that unlike beaver infants, who take instantly to water, young otters must be coaxed to swim. I remembered reading that the mother otter lets her babies play over her and climb on her back, then swims out from shore, taking them with her. She submerges suddenly, leaving the cubs to flounder and squeak—and learn to swim.

The cubs I watched were exhibiting the result of such spartan training as they darted and rolled in the water, sometimes reversing their course in hairpin curves. Though their motions appeared to be made for sheer fun, there was another purpose behind their antics. These youngsters needed practice in the art of finding food before they could be entirely independent of their parents. Whenever one of the parents came up with a large fish in his mouth, both offspring moved in for their share. The fish would be placed on a stump, and with his body half-submerged the adult otter sat up like a human being at a dining-room table. As he tore off bits of fish, his children grabbed pieces and chewed voraciously, raising their noses skyward from time to time like chickens taking a drink.

Sometimes the whole family made forays among the stranded lilies, perhaps hunting crustaceans, frogs, or turtles. As they humped along, the lily pads jumped and swayed over their backs. Accompanying the otters would be half a dozen green herons, who hopped as close as cowbirds to a cow while the otters fed. These crow-sized birds, standing erect as penguins, were intent on insects flushed by the lively otters and were also snatching leavings. The otters paid no attention to them, even when the brash birds whisked morsels from under their chins.

I was pleased when the larger of the adult otters (whom I assumed to be the father) turned and began swimming back toward me. Holding my breath, I crouched behind the briers as he came within fifteen feet and passed behind a screen of maples growing out of the dam. I thought he would slide over the dam, but he returned to his family and led them up toward the central lodge where the beavers, beleaguered by drought, were then staying. I felt a twinge of alarm. Would there be a tragic invasion?

Just then a late-roving beaver kit, not yet three months old, ambled over the dam in front of me and headed in the direction of the lodge. A moment later a second young beaver emerged from the lodge and started swimming toward the otters on a collision course. Here surely was a test of the otter-beaver relationship. If the otters were hungry for beaver, they had only to choose between two tempting—and extremely vulnerable—dishes. On tenterhooks, I watched the drama before me, glad that Cavit was not there with a shotgun. My laissez faire attitude toward nature did not always sit well with him, and he might have felt it his duty to blast the otters, on the assumption that they were about to attack the beaver kits.

The beaver from the lodge approached the otters and without the slightest hesitation swam through their midst. The otter family completely ignored him and continued their gliding progress up the stream. The two beavers met, touched noses, and dived together to bring up some lily roots, which they ate sitting in the water.

Daily thereafter I watched the otter family feed along the channel. Our accidental encounters had evidently given them confidence in me, as I had either remained still or had quietly withdrawn. No longer did they hurry out of sight as they used to do; instead, they snorted and retreated a little way, then detoured around me to come out in full view again. Their idea of a safe distance grew noticeably shorter.

One morning at six I lay hidden behind the curtain of greenbriers at the main dam. A heavy mist rolled off the channel, in ironic contrast to the cracked waste of mud and brittle stubble all around. The air, which would become so hot at midday, chilled me to the bone. Already the otters were stirring at the first bend of the channel, 150 feet away. For fifteen minutes I watched them tacking lazily back and forth like sailboats at the whim of fitful breezes, sometimes coming halfway to me, then moving back upstream. The cubs were playing king-of-the-castle on the roots of a twisted cedar stump. Now and then they crawled onto the bank to explore the water lilies, which sprawled everywhere. Once the cubs held a wrestling match on shore, causing quite a disturbance among the tangled lily stems.

Suddenly, next to me appeared another otter family, a lone

parent with three young. They had come over the dike and dived into a pool crowded with stranded fish. With a swish the otters went after the fish, eating a few before continuing their trek upstream. The two otter families were about to meet. Some tales I had read characterized otters as "fierce," and the impression left by such accounts made me expect a free-for-all should two families find themselves occupying the same fishing grounds.

With visible eagerness, they hurried toward each other, and when they met they touched noses. This was a rare nugget of otter lore for me, but there was more to come. For ten minutes the two families cavorted amiably, the children playing five-man games and the adults looping in and out with an air of abandon. And while the otters were intermingling in this sociable fashion, a young beaver swam calmly through their midst.

Then the two groups separated, swimming in opposite directions. My familiar otter pair with their two cubs swam right past me, not bothering to detour when they saw me. As they slipped through the sweet peppers at the end of the dam just twenty feet away, I gleefully hummed, "Getting to know you . . . ."

No sooner had they vanished among the weeds below than the other otter family in the pond reversed their course and were now coming my way. Through binoculars I watched them zigzagging and loitering along the stream, stopping every minute or so to climb out and frolic on the bank or sit on a stump nibbling a fish they had caught.

A great blue heron was standing near one stump, his six-inch beak poised like a spear. Several times I had seen his neck snake out, the spear plunge, and the beak come up holding a fish. He would eat the fish solemnly, his stately mien contrasting with the undignified lump in his throat as the fish went down. He would then take a sip of water, froth out his gray plumes, and resume his rigid stance.

As the frolicsome otters came up to where he stood in knee-deep water, they began to play at his feet. He loomed above them

At full speed, otter churns water prodigiously

like a stern schoolmaster overseeing mischievous pupils. Twice I saw him take a step or two toward the otters, but he never threatened them with his beak.

Half an hour later the otters had moved down to the final bend, only sixty feet from me. Three half-grown wood ducklings who were feeding close by scuttled off, wings flailing water, at their approach. They looked easy prey for the otters. After the first scurry the ducklings resumed feeding, while the otters passed without showing any interest and wriggled over the dam to their shaded haunts below. Reluctantly I went back to the kitchen and finished the breakfast dishes. By then it was ten o'clock.

Each contact with the otters added to my knowledge and at the same time sharpened my desire to know more. It was intriguing to learn the many ways in which these animals differed from the beavers, though both occupied the same territory and lived aquatic lives. For example, I never saw a lost beaver, but I did see lost otters. In the days to come, I was to find desperate otter parents hunting their strayed offspring and lost cubs searching for parents with frantic cries. This seemed strange, for not only do otters have an excellent communication system, but they usually travel as a close-knit family unit. Whether gliding back and forth or diving and emerging, the group moves in tight formation, with the cubs sandwiched between the parents. All the while, the parents emit mellow, ducklike quackings, and the young respond with soft chirps. Their subdued conversation reminds me of the buzz of communal bees or the voices of young quail with their parents.

The yip of a forsaken otter cub is a sound to remember. While getting lunch one day, I heard a series of piercing cries which meant an otter cub in trouble. Going out on the porch, I placed the cries at the main dam. Could one of the young, in climbing over, have gotten caught among the timbers? As I ran along the dike, I could still hear the distressed yipping, not unlike the cries of an unhappy puppy, but with the startling pitch of a birdcall.

Like many wild voices it was highly ventriloqual; and as I neared the dam, the voice seemed to come from the pond itself. I gazed out over the noon-bright water but could not see a ripple. Nor did I catch sight of a tiny, round gray head. Concentrating, I again thought the sound came from the dam, and clambering down, I looked for a cub trapped among the firmly meshed sticks. The cry came again, and this time I knew it was definitely not from the area of the dam. I looked once more across the pond. There, not ten feet away, was a small otter, head held high, treading water and looking around desperately. His yelps pierced my ears.

"Where's your mother?" I asked him, echoing his own question. He looked at me as I spoke, sprang toward me, then with a quick flip dived out of sight. In a moment he surfaced, twenty feet farther along the dike, and again gazed around him, crying wildly for help.

I could not help him. Three times he came back and looked me over, yipping piteously, but each time he turned away, to dive and come up farther away. Where on earth was his mother, that she could not hear such screams? Then I remembered how obstreperous one's offspring can be. He had probably disobeyed her and was now yelling for help. What was *I* to do? I did not even know his address.

Just as my maternal nerves were frayed almost to breaking, there came a commotion at the dike 200 feet away, just beyond where the cub was now surfaced. Waves buckled the water and a gray form cut the waves. The cries ended in mid-yip as the little otter streaked through the water to his mother; then the two slithered over the dike into the bushes and were gone. I was disappointed that the little one had not come to me as he had seemed on the verge of doing. I would have liked to cuddle a forlorn, wet otter cub in my arms.

A few days later I witnessed another lost-otter incident.

Cavit and I were sitting with the beavers at their evening

meal. At that time we were still feeding them at the main dam, for our front-yard cove was dry. The otter family came galloping over the dike and swam up the channel, where they started feeding a hundred feet away. Suddenly I saw a youngster swimming rapidly all around Whiskers, who sat eating in her usual tranquil manner. As the young one circled the big beaver, I was not sure whether it was a beaver kit or an otter cub. Counting beaver noses, I found that all five beaver kittens were at our feet.

Then I heard a high-pitched yelp, and recognizing it as that of a lost otter cub, I observed Whiskers's reaction. Staid as a sphinx, she kept on stripping bark and chewing, not even giving a motherly lunge toward the youngster, as she would have done to a beaver kit who annoyed her. Dipping in and out, yipping in a frenzy every time he came to the water's surface, the baby stayed close to Whiskers, evidently mistaking her for the mother he had lost. His cries could be heard all over the pond, yet the otter family continued making their way upstream, leisurely feeding as they went. After a few moments, disillusioned by Whiskers's indifference, the cub stopped crying, swam uncertainly a short distance, then speeded to catch up with his family.

I learned not to worry about vagrant young otters, for I had dramatic proof one day that though the mother otter teaches independence, she is alert to the welfare of her young. I was busy in the kitchen when I heard otters chirping. Wondering what it was this time, I found two otter cubs exploring the near shore just outside the cove. Screening myself behind a honeysuckle tangle, I peered out to where they were dipping among the lilies and wild rice, not twenty feet away, now and then holding up periscopelike heads tufted with bristles and giving companionable chirps of pleasure and discovery. The otter family, I had read, stayed together for a whole year. Then what were these two doing on their own?

Before long I saw an adult otter swimming frantically far out in the pond, head high, looking this way and that and holding her tail straight in the air. Back and forth she swam, 300 feet away, while these rascals dallied among the lilies. Eventually, either their playful chirps reached her ears or she otherwise sensed them, for she veered abruptly and charged straight toward them, uttering excited snorts. As she came near, the young ones hurried to meet her, and the three went undulating off.

Although the pond was ideal for otter watching, I decided to go downstream to where the otter had barked at me as I was investigating the water situation during the drought. (I now thought of this place as Otter Landing.) I believed he had a den there, possibly with young in it. Frequently, just after dark, I had seen greenish eyes gleaming as otters, swimming upstream, passed the feeding beavers. About ten in the morning the otters usually slipped over the dam on their way back down the stream. Assuming they were hunting for food or gamboling about all night, where did they spend the day? I was determined to find out.

One morning, stepping carefully so as not to advertise my approach, I made my way to Otter Landing. I took a seat on the bank directly opposite the landing and waited. Soon, a heavy body approached from upstream, sending ripples ahead to lap the shore. Though the ripples were big enough to have been made by an otter, it was only Greenbrier, who swam slowly, looking up at me, then lazily turned and dived into a hole in the bank just above one of his dams. After a few minutes he reappeared. He then gave a few hissing sniffs, as though he was suspicious. I spoke to him in a low voice so the otters would not be disturbed, and he went back under the bank. In a few seconds he was out again, with a big mouthful of mud, roots, and twigs, which he pushed against the dam and tucked firmly into place with fingers and nose. Either my presence made him uneasy or this was just another of his two-minute maintenance jobs, for he left then to swim back upstream. For an hour I sat without moving, but no otter appeared on the landing. I did see one, however, treading back and forth in the underbrush beyond the landing, chirping all the time. He was evidently disturbed by my presence.

The next day, after lunch, I went back, and sitting down on the bank, peered intently into the bushes where I had seen the otter the day before. I noticed a log I did not remember seeing. On closer inspection, it looked very much like a sleeping otter. Focusing my eyes more sharply, I saw an almost imperceptible movement and then was able to make out the forms of several otters lolling together in the dry leaves of the forest floor. Sunlight flickered over them through the leaves of tall maples.

I watched and waited. Every sound was clear in the stillness— the rustle of a bird in a treetop, the hammering of our neighbor on his house, the whine of an insect. Now and then one of the otters stirred, shifting his position or flipping off flies with his round webbed hands. Each time one moved, the puzzle of their intertwined shapes became clearer, until I finally could distinguish a family of four. They were sprawled on their backs, revealing the rich tan patches on their throats. Each movement they made caused a frond of sweet pepper to quiver above them.

Because I kept expecting the otters to get up at any moment, I crouched as though hypnotized, hour after hour. Now and then they would wriggle, wave a paw, or raise a sleek head in a yawn. It was nearly dark before I left, and still the otters slumbered on. Though somewhat disgruntled at the length of their nap, and perforce my stay, I was happy to have discovered their sleeping place. Now my plan was clear. Early in the morning I would come to watch them prepare for sleep; just before sunset I would try to observe them waking up and starting their nightly rounds.

At 6:30 the following morning, I went stealthily back to the same place. The sun was just rising as I stood across from the landing. The otters were not there. I was disappointed, but just then I heard a noise at an upstream bend and saw that the water was roiled. Otters? No, again it was Greenbrier. He came swimming slowly around the bend with a load of mud for his dam. At the same time I caught sight of a young beaver scrambling onto Otter Landing, and another swimming in the stream. The water at the bend churned once more, and from that direction came a sharp bark. Into sight came the otter family, headed downstream.

One of the otter cubs yapped a greeting, rushed onto the landing, and began to chase the beaver kitten who had been sitting there. The surprised kitten, after a few clumsy gambols, slid down the bank into the water. The cub followed, and a melee ensued between the four youngsters, as they played tag on the surface and underwater, giving each other friendly nudges and sniffles. While the otter cubs yipped and chirped with excitement, the beavers' attitude seemed one of good-natured tolerance of such boisterousness.

Through it all Greenbrier methodically continued to shore up his dam, and the otter parents, long and agile, looped smoothly about the pool or ran up along the shore before sliding back into the water. Soon the otter family moved on down the stream, not pausing, as I had hoped, at their well-worn landing. As the high-pitched voices of the otter cubs came from far down the stream, the two beaver kits climbed onto Otter Landing, and seating themselves on their tails, began the leisurely rite of fur combing.

Every few days I found time to scout Otter Landing and often discovered the otters asleep, but my evening visits proved unsuccessful. On the nights I watched they snoozed till after dark. Finally, one evening I managed to catch them awake. I was on my way down to the landing when I met Whiskers en route to the feeding place at the pond. As was her custom, she was abroad early and had left the kittens behind. She was standing half-submerged in shallow water, and around her a group of otters cavorted in the mud. Whiskers seemed bewildered by so much activity, hampered as she was by the narrowness of the channel, which was bordered there by wide margins of mud. The otters

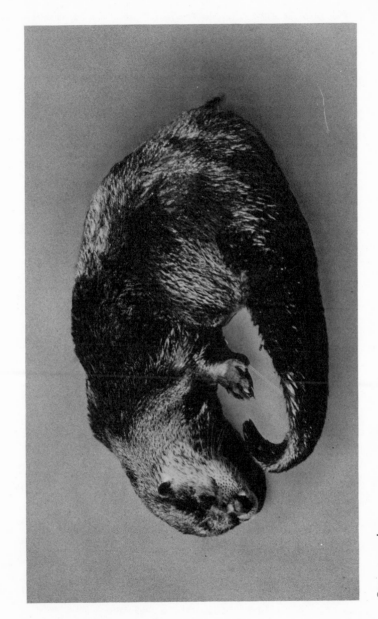

Otter snoozing

must have seen me, for with swaying heads and a few chirps they left us. Saying hello to Whiskers, I hurried after them to Otter Landing but could not catch up. Their high-pitched barks came from farther and farther away down the stream.

At the landing I came on beavers galore, all this season's kittens. Nipper was sitting on a log next to the landing eating, when Fluffy the Second, the most arrogant, climbed up beside him and either waddled clumsily into him or pushed him on purpose. Nipper tumbled off the log and landed in the water upside down. When he came up, he was still holding onto his stick and eating. Then these two kittens began to wrestle and dive all over the pool. Blondie, Brownie, and Clipper were swimming around, now and then nibbling on sweet-pepper stems and leaves, which they cut off along the shore. Greenbrier was still working on his dam.

Before darkness settled, I returned to the dam, where Whiskers, a truant from her family, was still at her hearty poplar breakfast. Though she had long ago weaned the kittens, she still seemed to have the biggest appetite of all. She was very confiding that evening, apparently unruffled by her encounter with the otters. When she had finished eating, she stepped close to me, heaved herself upright, and began combing her fur. Her broad back was only a foot from my knee, and I was tempted to put out my hand and pet her but was afraid she might interpret such a move as hostile. After a thorough grooming, she turned toward me, daintily gnawed off a leafy twig from the branch I was holding, and carried it into the water. Meanwhile, the five babies had come and were tugging at sticks, mewing in protest when a sibling came too near, and carting off huge portions to eat in separate corners. One greedy kit waddled up to a branch and gnawed off one twig at a time until he had a mouthful, which he carried under an overhanging ledge to eat. He looked like a dressmaker holding pins in her teeth.

Not long after this, in mid-September, I met the otters again. At seven one morning I was seated opposite Otter Landing, still hoping to watch an otter bedtime. No beavers or otters were in sight. From dense cedars beyond me the voice of a wood thrush purled, and a Maryland yellowthroat, bright against the dark mud, leaned from the dam to take a drink. I heard snatches of alien song from unidentified warblers passing through on migration. The minutes lengthened.

I was about to leave when the otters arrived. They paused before me, and three glossy gray youngsters climbed onto the log where I had seen the baby beavers. All three posed there for a few minutes, yawning and stretching like sleepy cats. Then they dived into the water and whirled about the pool, chirping constantly. The mother came toward me and from ten feet away stared intently. I stared right back, feeling quite *de trop,* but determined to brazen it out. Either she accepted me as part of the scenery, or she decided that I was a harmless neighbor. Giving a soft signal to her young, she sent them into the hole in the bank, then followed them in, without any sign of alarm. They all emerged among the maples, where they shook their fur and toweled themselves in the leaves. They did not lie down, however; much to my disappointment they moved away through the underbrush, where I heard them rustling and chirping for some time. Evidently they were mistrustful of my presence, after all.

The following morning the other otter family came, parents quacking and young chirping musically as they swam in one snakelike formation to their hole in the bank. Clambering over the log, one parent and the cubs went in, while the other parent remained, watching alertly, eyes directed my way. Whether he saw me or not, I can not be sure, but he soon turned and followed the others. Emerging on the far shore, all four rolled and tumbled in the leaves at the roots of the maples, then lay down in a close-knit tangle to sleep. Tiptoeing away, I left them.

I telephoned Al to tell him that the drought had given him the chance of a lifetime to photograph otters. He arrived the next afternoon, and in the center of the pond, on caked mud along the channel, he set up his burlap blind just sixty feet from a giant cedar stump where the otter cubs usually played. Before daylight the next morning I started for the blind so that I would arrive ahead of the otters. Al would come later with his camera, and then I would leave, giving any otters who might be near the impression that the blind was empty.

In the moonlight preceding dawn I walked over the desert of mud, where lily pads stood up crisply, freshened by the night's coolness. Each step made a crackle like crushed ice as stubble shattered beneath my feet. Reaching the blind, I crawled in and opened the peephole to get a view up the channel. Half an hour later, the otters came around the curve, dipping and rearing and loitering along the shores.

Suddenly an otter's whiskery face appeared near the stump opposite me. His snub nose gave a snuffle, then he began to chirp very softly, turning his head this way and that. He dipped his head under, blowing bubbles, then raised up, and with water streaming off him, clambered over the stump, exposing his whole sinuous length. Lifting his nose, he tested the air before wiggling back down the way he had come and hurrying off to meet the others, who were moving closer.

Daylight was still to come, but roosters crowed, a song sparrow sang, a cardinal began to call, and the twittering of other birds increased. Killdeer skittered close, and with a whir of wings a flock of red-winged blackbirds wheeled and landed on the mud, to probe industriously for insects among the lily pads. At last I heard the crunch of Al's feet; the sound seemed very loud. I was fearful that the otters, now only 200 feet away, might take alarm and leave.

But they stayed. Bounding along the shore and diving into the pool for brief swims, the otters were gradually coming nearer. Al got his equipment into the blind, and I tiptoed back across the dry pond. By the time I had reached the shore, the otters were only a pebble's toss from the blind.

Preparing breakfast in the kitchen, I glanced out every few minutes. The sky was light gray, paling the moon. Soon the sun would rise and shine full on the pond. As we all sat down at the table, Cavit said, "How'd it go?"

"Fine. They're at the blind now, and the light will be good in a few minutes. He can't miss."

The sun showed red beyond the forest, but I noticed white fog thick as cotton rolling up along the channel. Although in New Jersey our brightest days are often heralded by fog, I was a little worried. The otters might leave before the fog lifted.

"They'll stay there," said Cavit. "They always do."

"It's a good chance," Ned reminded me. "You always said otters like misty days."

So my family rallied around. After awhile a plane zoomed over, skimming the top of the fog. We were still at the breakfast table when a tap came at the door. Al was back. He plodded in, carrying his equipment, and slumped into a chair, a twisted grin on his face. Wrapping cold hands around a hot cup of coffee, he told us his story.

"Got everything set up, and it was beautiful. If they came to that stump, I was in. Looked out that peephole and saw 'em coming, making that little quack they do. Those cubs climbed right up on the stump. One of the old ones hauled out a big fish and started eating right across from me. I could have gotten a dozen pictures, but there wasn't any light yet."

Al glanced around the table, still that funny hurt look on his face. He took a sip of coffee, then blurted out, "Doggone! Wish I'd had a gun. I'd have taken a shot at that guy!"

He sat quiet after this outburst, prolonging the suspense. Then he looked up. "The darn fog rolled in, but I knew that would pass. The sun was just coming over the treetops, and in five minutes I'd have had perfect light. The otters didn't even know I was there. I was all set for the moon.

"Then that busy little plane had to come over. He zoomed

down real close—buzzing the blind, I guess. The otters were scared. I heard the big ones snort; then they all dived in and beat it. They rushed clear down over the dam."

"Didn't you get anything?"

"The light wasn't right yet. When I saw they were scared, I took two fast ones, but they won't be any good." They were not; and before Al could try again the rain came, flooding the pond. We took down the blind.

The rain began at noon, and at six that evening I walked next to the stream, eager to share the beavers' and otters' joy. Rain poured down through thrashing branches as I waded along a path six inches underwater. At the place where Whiskers had waded in mud and met the otters, the narrow stream had broadened suddenly to a width of three feet. The raindrops were big, creating thousands of bubbles on the surface of the water. Each flurry of bubbles looked like an approaching otter, but no otters came, and neither did the beavers. Apparently both were celebrating elsewhere.

By morning the stream had risen until the lodge entrances were covered and water was pouring over the dam above Otter Landing. Waiting there, I heard a series of loud splashes below the next dam. I tiptoed down the path and around the bend. There three young beavers were sitting on the bank combing their fur in their characteristic Buddhalike pose, while the other two were busy cutting off tender sweet-pepper bushes. Screened by brush, I watched until Whiskers came swimming past. All five youngsters flung themselves after her, some almost on her tail, and followed her out of sight down the stream.

Once more we put poplar above the main dam, and it did not take the beavers long to find the new source of supply. So in early October I began another period of carefree beaver watching. It was good to see shining water where dry mud had lain so long and to watch a revived nature's increased activity. A kingfisher called from a stub over the water. Flickers drummed.

High overhead wheeled a red-tailed hawk, spiraling in wide arcs against stacked cumulous clouds. Frogs sang now as in springtime, and even a few toads trilled. The freshened woods were filled with migrating woodpeckers, warblers, towhees, and whippoor-wills, some giving faint echoes of their spring musical perfor-mances. Brown thrashers and catbirds fed on a giant pokeweed, which luxuriated over the lodge, just below the main dam, where the beavers were now staying. At my feet I could see the gleam of swimming fish, and the sun shone on the wake of otters as they moved up and down the pond. Often I heard the barking and chirping of the irrepressible cubs; for though Otter Landing was flooded and the otters stayed elsewhere, they still passed up and down the stream daily. Al built a blind at the dam, which they were in the habit of crossing, and prepared to get pictures.

In the days to come I witnessed many meetings of beaver and otter families which convinced me that Emil Liers of Minnesota was right when he said, "Otters who burrow into a beaver lodge are often after crustaceans. If a beaver is killed by an otter it is the exception to the rule."

At each otter sighting Cavit would mutter, "There goes an otter rubbing his stomach. One less beaver kitten, you'll see." But every time we counted, the five kittens were still there.

Grey Owl and Others

DURING THE MONTHS when the mere sight of a beaver was a thrill, I read and reread Grey Owl's book *Pilgrims of the Wild*. His contacts with beavers inspired me, and growing intimacy with our beavers gave the book new meaning each time I read it. And later, Cavit and I, like Grey Owl and his wife, Anahareo, pledged to make the beavers' safety our responsibility.

Born in 1888 in Canada, of Scotch and Indian parentage, Grey Owl spent his early years in England but then returned to Canada. He took part in the Cobalt silver rush of 1905 as canoeman and packer. The Ojibway tribe of Indians who adopted him named him Grey Owl because of his nighttime wanderings. He learned their language, lived their nomadic life, and from them derived his forest lore. Although he was a trapper, living among a people who depended on trapping for their survival, he finally gave it up to devote his life to the conservation of the fast-dwindling wildlife.

Grey Owl and his Mohawk Indian bride, Anahareo, were living in the bush, where they ate, slept, and dreamed traplines. But Anahareo became more and more revolted by the cruelty of trapping, and as her unhappiness deepened, her husband began to think. "Always I had pitied," wrote Grey Owl, "but had closed my mind to all thoughts of compassion save in retrospect."

One spring, when they went to town to sell their winter's fur catch, Grey Owl and Anahareo found prices so low that they could not pay off their debt. In spite of his reluctance to trap beavers when the young were in the lodges, Grey Owl decided to do so. He caught a mother beaver, who escaped but later died, leaving two kittens. As the small waifs came to the surface looking for their mother, Anahareo begged Grey Owl to save them. So they took the kittens home, "two funny-looking furry creatures with little scaly tails and exaggerated hind feet, that weighed less than a half a pound apiece, and that tramped sedately up and down the bottom of the canoe with that steady, persistent, purposeful walk that we were later to know so well."

Feeding the kittens canned milk, later supplemented by porridge and bannock, the couple raised the orphans. In doing so, they found all their preconceived ideas about wild animals upset. The little beavers did not cringe terror-stricken in a corner. Instead, fastening themselves enthusiastically on their protectors, they demanded unceasing attention.

"They were very gentle," wrote Grey Owl, "and they had a kind of naive disarming friendliness of disposition that took it quite for granted that they belonged, and that we were well disposed towards them and would see them through."

The babies were inseparable, even sleeping with a tight hold on the other's fur, until they learned to creep into bed with their human guardians, each cuddling up to his favorite. Clean and good-natured, they were welcome bedmates, and their appealing ways soon touched a chord of such tenderness in Grey Owl that he was afraid his feelings would compromise his chief means of livelihood—the beaver hunt.

He wrote: "I found it strange and a little disquieting that these animals, that had seemed heretofore to have only one use, and that I had destroyed by hundreds, should turn out to be so likeable, should so arouse the protective instinct of a man who was their natural enemy.

"From a purely economic viewpoint, I had long been opposed to the wholesale slaughter now going forward, which was indeed almost at an end for want of victims. But this was different. These beasts had feelings and could express them very well; they could talk, they had affection, they knew what it was to be happy, to be lonely—why, they were little people! And they must be all like that. All this tallied with the incredible stories I had heard in younger days, and perhaps accounted for the veneration that our people, when savage, had held them in, calling them 'Beaver People,' 'Little Indians,' and 'Talking Brothers.' Indian mothers, bereaved of an infant, had suckled baby beavers at their breasts and thus gained some solace. I had seen them myself cared for tenderly by those whose hands they had fallen into. And I would have left them to die with never a thought, an intention that seemed now to have been something nearly barbarous."

Musing on the past, Grey Owl wrote: "The exuberant recklessness of my earlier days was past and gone, those lonely, wild and heedless days in the vast and empty silences, when I had been sufficient unto myself, leaving death behind me everywhere. I was beginning to ponder more and more deeply on the unfairness and injustice of trapping these animals. The influx of hordes of incompetent amateur trappers that high fur prices had inflicted on the country, I had looked on with uneasiness for some years past as a menace to the profession, and had constantly deplored the brutality of their methods. The regular trapper, if he knows his business at all, sets for beaver only under the ice, so the animal is invariably and cleanly drowned, or else escapes the trap uninjured. A dead animal, decently killed was no great matter, but a crippled beast was a crime and the woods were full of them.

"A number of incidents had contributed to this line of thought. About the first of these was the sight of a mother beaver nursing one of her kittens whilst fast by one foot in a trap. She was moaning with pain, yet when I liberated her, minus a foot, she waited nearby for the tardy and inquisitive kitten, seeming by her actions to realize that she had nothing to fear from me. Suspended in the air by a spring-pole, I found another female—a beast that cried out in a voice strangely human when I took her down, and died with one of my fingers tightly grasped in her uninjured paw. She had been about to become a mother. This spring-pole is a particularly fiendish contrivance that jerks the unfortunate creature out of the water to hang there. The animal is uninjured and may remain there for days until it dies of thirst and exhaustion. Frequently birds will pick out the eyes before the animal is dead. These and other methods equally brutal are adopted by unskilled hunters who can get their beaver no other way, and these instances were only two out of dozens to be seen on every hand.

"These inhumanities aroused in me a strange feeling; it was that these persecuted creatures no longer appeared to me as lawful prey, but as co-dwellers in this wilderness that was being so despoiled, the wilderness that was so relentless yet so noble an antagonist. They too fought against its hardships and made their home in it; we all, man and beast, were comrades-in-arms. To see them so abused awoke in me a kind of loyalty or *esprit-de-corps,* so that for me to continue my own operations against them along with these alien interlopers who had nothing in common with any of us, now seemed like some form of treason almost as though I were a renegade who assisted an invader to despoil his unarmed fellow-country men . . . .

"The little beavers are born any time from the middle of May to the first week in June. Beaver hides are still prime at that season in Northern areas. So the Spring hunt is still on, and transients swept through the country like a relentless scourge, invading the territories of others, killing off the mother beaver who are easily caught at that time, and passed on to fresh fields leaving the baby beavers to starve by hundreds. Apart from the barbarity of this method, it had done more in a decade to annihilate the beaver than the Winter trapping of centuries. Often the woe-begone little creatures, already some time without food, would attempt to follow the hunter's canoe as he paddled away with the body of their mother, wailing despairfully but ineffectually. It is to be said in favour of natives that they nearly always adopted these orphans. But their story had always been pitiful, even to the apathetic Indians—a craving for attention, a clutching of little forepaws, confinement, neglect, and after a few weeks almost inevitable death, wailing to the last, with unforgettable voices that seemed somehow to yet be faintly audible long after they were still and the little thwarted lives had passed into the discard.

"I had rescued a number myself. I remember one little fellow, who used to sleep rolled up in a furry ball on the side of my head, all night; and when I turned over he would awaken, and passing across my forehead as I rolled, would arrive at the other side all set, there to fall asleep again. He used to climb up on my shoulder, and as I worked around, cooking or whatnot, he would lie draped across the back of my neck and I often ate my meals with him there. But he was a sick little beaver, and became at last too weak to do these things and died one day in my hand, still trying feebly to climb up to his old familiar place.

"Two others were with me for three weeks and were exceptionally playful and chummy, and could not bear to be three feet apart. They used to follow me around, tight to my heels, coaxing plaintively to be noticed, until they too, suddenly drooped and died. Right to the last they had their tiny paws clutched in each other's fur, as though to be sure they were not parted even on this the last of all their journeyings.

"I had watched fat little beavers sitting up like queer diminutive Buddhas on a river bank, solemnly wagging their heads at the rising sun, while the mother lay by and crooned at them, plucking them towards her at intervals and rolling on her back from time to time, murmuring with contentment, happy with her young and the sheer joy of living.

"The spectacle of a crippled beaver with only one hind leg and three stumps, doing his best to carry on, had moved me to put him out of his misery. Every year in March, when they sometimes came out on the surface, I had laid in wait for beaver and killed them with a club, and their resignation in the face of death was always disturbing; some of them had tried to shelter their heads from the blow with their hands. One, badly wounded with shot, had swam ashore within a few feet of me, and had lain there looking up at me so that I had boggled the execution most horribly. The incident had haunted me for days.

"I was getting sick of the constant butchery, and the sight of the ruined works so toilsomely erected, the accusing loneliness of the empty beaver ghost-towns, and the utter desolation of the ravaged colonies was saddening to any thinking man. But this had not, however, prevented me from going on to the next lodge and setting my traps as carefully as ever; and like many another good business man I had justified myself, and had resolutely closed my mind to any thought of the hardships I might be inflicting in the course of my profitable undertakings. They had seemed to me to be just foolish dupes who took my proffered lures, beasts that were put on earth for my convenience, dumb brutes that didn't know the difference. And now had come these small and willing captives, with their almost child-like intimacies and murmurings of affection, their rollicking good fellowship with not only each other but ourselves, their keen awareness, their air of knowing what it was all about. They seemed to be almost like little folk from some other planet, whose language we could not yet quite understand. To kill such creatures seemed monstrous. I would do no more of it. Instead of persecuting them further I would study them, see just what there really was to them. I perhaps could start a colony of my own; these animals could not be permitted to pass completely from the face of this wilderness. I thought of Michael Pablo and the buffalo. His idea had borne fruit: why should not mine? But this matter took some figuring. There was nothing simple about it. I had first to discover a family of beaver not already claimed by some other hunter, and then hold them against comers, by no means an easy task. I would tame them; so far an unheard of proceeding, but I had faith in the crazy scheme, and was convinced by what I knew of our little fellows that this was possible. It was like to be a hungry, thankless job, unless I could locate in a good fur country that would provide us a livelihood, in which case it would swarm with trappers and I would have to be my own game warden, with consequent and highly unpleasant antagonisms. I would undoubtedly be looked on as a renegade; but my mind was made up, and I would attempt to go through with it.

"Meanwhile my equipment consisted of two small beaver and a bill at the grocery store."

With some misgivings, Grey Owl broke the news to Anahareo, informing her that he was done with beaver hunting for good. At first she could not believe it, but Grey Owl insisted that he meant what he said. He told her his plans, adding that it might go hard with them—they might have to pull in their belts a few notches. "Are you game?" he asked.

"Of course," she said. "We'll both work at it."

That was the beginning of their "Pilgrimage." They built their House of McGinnis (the beaver kittens were named McGinty and McGinnis for their industrious Irish ways), and it was there that Grey Owl first conceived the idea of writing about his experiences. While the elflike beaver kittens hopped and capered about the cabin, building their own "lodge" beneath the bunk, he began the work which was to save Canada's beavers from extinction and make his own name known around the world.

Our dream was as quixotic as Grey Owl's. He had worked toward his goal through every difficulty, and Cavit and I could do the same. It was our dream to see deserted lodges thrive and sparkling water flow over dams all up and down New Jersey streams, where now only isolated pairs of beavers made occasional oases in a barren waste. The sanctuary Grey Owl and Anahareo established in the Canadian wilderness emboldened me to keep on trying to lure our beavers.

I discovered that Grey Owl was right about beavers being highly individualistic. Their taste in food was one example. While our beavers refused to eat apples, pancakes, potatoes, or bread—all of which beavers are supposed to like—Nipper, one of the kits, took to eating shelled corn. We saw him dive in the cove, come up with a single kernel in his fingers, eat it, and then go down for more. The rest of the family never touched corn. The following year, however, two-month-old Clipper emulated his big brother. With a flip of his black tail he dived in and came up with his own kernel of corn. From that time on, the two dived side by side, their big and little tails almost touching.

Grey Owl's experiences helped us, not only with beaver lore, but in our bewildering contacts with people who looked on the project of a wildlife refuge as a very foolish scheme. Like him, I wrote about my nature observations in the refuge. I began a ten-page newsletter called "Good News," which I distributed as widely as I could and especially tried to get into schools.

One beautiful fall day, with swamp maples and sour gums blazing scarlet through bright green foliage, I drove the children out to the school bus. A light mist was lifting. Across the road in front of us hurried a red squirrel carrying a pinecone in his mouth. A cottontail veered into rusty bracken along the side. Passing under the bustling white-faced hornets' nest hung from an oak branch, we turned onto Unexpected Road.

Opposite our mailbox a red sports car was parked. On my way home, I got out to slip a leaflet through the car door handle. The leaflet, "A New Look at Sportsmanship," was one I had had published. In the back seat of the car lay a quiver of arrows, shafts tipped with gay feathers. Bow-hunting season had begun that morning, and as promptly as conscientious workers punching a clock, the hunters had arrived. I knew that they were either perched high on a wooden stand or crouched hidden along a well-traveled deer trail in the woods behind our neighbor's cabin.

Near noon I walked out with Junior to get the mail. There sat the bow hunters, eating lunch. They were young fellows, in their early twenties, dressed in camouflage clothes of green and brown. The boy facing me, looking hearty and well-fed, chewed his sandwich with relish, cap pushed back over thick brown hair. The other, tall and spare, was eating more slowly. In his left hand he held my hunting pamphlet, which he was reading aloud as he ate. In his belt was thrust a long-bladed knife with fancy horn handle. He looked up at me from behind dark-rimmed glasses. "Good morning," he said genially and smiled at Junior, who was sniffing the lunch bag appreciatively, while the other boy patted him on the head.

"I see you got my message," I said, indicating the pamphlet.

He laughed. "Yes. You've got quite a lot to say here."

"I love to hunt," the plump boy said, pushing his cap farther back on his head. "You'd never get me to give up hunting. It's a great sport."

"Sport?" I asked. "Sport to pick on defenseless animals?"

"Oh, you think I enjoy killing? I just love to be out in the woods matching wits with the animals."

I thought of Whiskers and her timorous "You won't hurt me, will you?" approach.

The tall young man said quickly, "You say the animals don't have a defense. A deer has all kinds of advantage. He can see better; he can run faster; his hearing is fantastic. Why, in bow hunting, you're lucky if you even get the bow up before he's gone, to say nothing of making a hit."

"That's not the point," I said. "The point is that you are out to kill him—if you can—but he's not out to kill you. What's sporting about that?"

"It's the thrill of the chase. Trying to outwit him on his own ground. I've played other sports—basketball, football. People get hurt there, even killed. Yet you call it sport."

"Yes, but if anyone gets hurt, it's an accident. Your motive is to play the game. Both sides know the rules, and you're supposed to be evenly matched."

"There you go again. The deer has all the advantage over the hunter. I've been out eleven years now, and I haven't gotten a deer yet. But I like being in the woods."

"Well, why not take a camera with you? I have friends who used to hunt, and they turned to wildlife photography. They say it's ten times more fun. You have to get closer, be in sharp focus."

"You can't let the deer multiply," he declared. "Have you ever seen a deer starve to death?"

"No."

"Well, I have. Lying there, all skin and bones. I like deer meat. I hate to see a deer lying dead of starvation when I could maybe have been enjoying the meat. With proper management, the deer are kept in control and that doesn't happen." He took off his camouflage cap and ran his hand over his close-cropped black hair.

"Who shot off all the wild predators?" I asked.

"Hunters, I suppose. But the predators are gone now. Man has to be the predator. Besides," and he looked over to the field next to the refuge, "the deer damage the crops." He swept his arm toward the field. "Ask your neighbor what the deer did to his sweet-potato crop last year."

"I know," I said. "They come to a crop as to bait, even from woods like ours, full of browse. That's why we're building a deer fence along the edge of the woods." I tried another tack. "Did you ever put yourself in the place of the deer?"

Both boys laughed aloud.

I looked at them, trying to understand their viewpoint. But the word "sport" stuck in my craw.

"Animals may have to be controlled," I went on. "But it should be done only when necessary—not for sport."

"The deer's going to get killed. Why not enjoy the sport? It's a contest. He has a chance for his life."

"Does he," I said, "when hunters set out piles of bait long before the season, so he'll get used to it? He eats and finds it safe. Then one morning he's ambushed from a tree. I'm sorry, but I can't see any contest. The whole point is that you're out to get him, but he's not out to get you. How can he cope with human ingenuity? Now, if you fellows like bow hunting, and you both agree to go into the woods and try to outwit each other, I'd call it fair sport."

They both grinned, exchanging glances.

"You think I'm a nut," I said, "but look. I live here with the animals year round. I see things from their viewpoint. How many people do you think come to these woods outside of hunting season, to study the animals? None. Yours is the first car I've seen here since last winter. During firearms deer season, you'll find fifty men in there, with their walkie-talkies, driving deer right toward this road where men are lined up waiting. The deer have got to go somewhere. It's like a slaughterhouse. How can you call it *sport?*"

"Well, you're talking about deer drives. I go after my deer alone. As I say, I don't want to hurt them." The tall one picked up his bow, which had been leaning against a tree. Pulling his cap down over his eyes, he began to rub his hand up and down the smooth wood. "Of course with an arrow, the deer's got to bleed to death, no matter where you hit him. But I'd follow him and finish him off." He stepped over to the car and reached into the trunk, bringing out a bunch of arrows with gaudy feathers and deadly cutting tips.

How could I get him to understand? "We have beavers," I said. "I've known them for years. Whiskers, the mother, has come up and talked to me and put her hand on my knee. You wouldn't kill a dog for sport, would you?"

"Of course not."

"You've got my point," I told him. "To me, the wild animals are just like a dog is to you. They're my friends. They could be your friends too if you'd let them. But to a trapper a beaver's just another pelt. He'd catch Whiskers or Greenbrier or one of their children—kill them, and never know what they're really like."

For a moment we stood quietly, while a light gust blew down a flurry of leaves. Then the tall young man began thrusting arrows into his quiver, and the round-faced one stooped to glean litter from the grass.

"As I said," the tall one repeated, "I haven't got a deer in eleven years. I've been out in all kinds of weather, year after year. I figure any deer I get, the little suffering he'd do wouldn't be much compared to what I've gone through to get him."

The next day, when I went to get the mail, the red car was again parked, but the boys were nowhere in sight. A scrap of cardboard lay caught in the weeds, and I reached down to pick it up. It was the backer from a pack of deer scent, and I read, "Nature's Appeal. Irresistible. Attracts All Deer." The package (priced at $2.50) guaranteed results, stating that the scent would eliminate the animal's caution, make him curious, and arouse his two most compelling natural instincts.

So much for fair play.

I told Ted Kiefer, our son's music teacher, about my talk with the bow hunters. Kiefer, an outdoorsman, was formerly a hunter. He had become uneasy about waiting over a deer trail, he told me. It seemed too much like an ambush. So he tried stalking. He put on sneakers and began creeping through the brush, wondering how close he could come to a deer. One day he came within ten feet of a doe, who was eating acorns. She did not raise her head.

"Seeing her like that—she didn't even know I was there!—I had no thought of nocking an arrow. She looked like a pet calf. When I told the fellows, they laughed at me. After that I did a lot of stalking and found it easy. But every time I came back empty-handed, the fellows made fun of me. After awhile I lost interest in hunting. It was more fun to watch the animals, and with those guys I couldn't even boast of what I'd seen."

"What finally made you quit hunting for good?" I asked.

"I was still going hunting when Lorraine and I were married. Then Lorraine took a course under Dr. Heinz Meng, the ornithologist. She was so enthusiastic that she'd take me back to the places where the class had gone on field trips. Here at home, we put up bird feeders and began to watch birds. Then one night I almost ran into a skunk—or he into me. Lorraine saw a possum eating persimmons under our tree, and raccoons started coming to our feeders. One morning I was looking at ducks on our creek when suddenly I saw two otters, who spent the morning fishing and playing. We had rabbits in the yard, and Lorraine had seen a fox out back. We began to realize what we had here.

"Meanwhile, I'd heard about your place. Lorraine was getting your newsletter, 'Good News.' Remember when I came over to look at the refuge? I met Al Francesconi over there and got interested in wildlife photography. That fall we posted Triple Oaks as a wildlife refuge, and that Christmas Lorraine gave me a camera. I was hooked."

Kiefer gave a slow, mischievous smile. "Speaking of your newsletter," he said, "I used to read every word. I was a hunter then, and each time I opened 'Good News' I'd say to myself, 'Wonder what the kook has to say this time?' Some of those things got to me; I had to admit they were right. But I was carrying on a little war with myself, trying not to give in."

I wondered how many hunters felt some of the same conflict.

A month later, we caught a hound in the refuge and dialed the number scratched on his collar. Mike Deflora answered the phone. "That's my dog," his voice quavered. "I'm comin' over. Hold onto him for me."

When he came, the conversation turned to hunting, and once again I asked, "Why?"

"I dunno. It's something to do outdoors. I like to hear the dogs."

"Couldn't you just hike?"

He fell back on a fifty-year-old dodge: "Well, you know, if we didn't hunt, animals would overrun us."

"How about the quail raised in pens?" I asked.

"That's a scandal!" he said, looking up from where he was fumbling with the dog's collar. "Why, you know it's our license money pays for them quail. The game man brings 'em down by truckload Friday night and lets 'em loose. Saturday morning I get up early, but somebody's always ahead of me. There's just not enough to go round."

"Don't you feel sorry for the quail?" I asked him.

"They're just birds," he said. "We eat 'em, you know. They're not wasted."

"But they want to live."

"We all do. But life is cruel. I tell you, ma'am, if everybody would stop hunting tomorrow, I'd be glad to."

"Well, couldn't you just stop killing quail, when they're so scarce?"

"Wouldn't do no good. If I don't get 'em, somebody else will. Why, ma'am, if you'd let people come in here"—he waved his hand around the refuge—"and charged 'em ten dollars apiece, you'd make a pile of money."

"But there's hardly anything here," I said.

"Don't matter," he said. "They'd pay—just for the chance."

I said no more. Mike collared his dog and led him to the truck. Climbing in stiffly, he sat for a moment, his gnarled hand on the dog's shoulder. "This here's my old pal," he said proudly. "We've hunted together for ten years."

I could never understand how anyone who loved a pet dog

could persecute other animals as a hobby. My work with young children, who expressed such deep concern for animals of all kinds, gave me hope that such an attitude might eventually be changed; but when I saw ten- or twelve-year-old boys glowing with pride on their first hunting excursions—the same boys who only a few years before had listened with such interest to my nature stories—I was discouraged. Tradition kept overpowering education.

Early in December firearms deer season began, and beaver watching had to be postponed to permit Cavit and me to constantly patrol our boundary lines, checking our signs and seeing that the fence had not been cut. That first morning, a Monday, we started our first patrol before dawn. The night had been bitter cold, and we bundled up against a sharp wind. It was barely light enough to see as we drove out, but we found cars and trucks already parked at the refuge borders. The hunters were in the adjoining woods.

As we made the final turn around the refuge and started down the last line of deer fence, Cavit shouted, "There's a fire!" Smoke was rising up ahead; it seemed to be coming from inside the refuge. Putting on speed, Cavit bounced the jeep along the rough track till we were near enough for a good look. We saw a fire crackling inside our deer fence. The stiff wind was carrying the flames rapidly into our woods, straight toward our house.

For years disgruntled hunters had been threatening to touch a match to our place, but we had never worried too much. That fall we had breathed more easily than usual, for the new stretch of seven-foot fence, designed to prevent crop damage by deer, would also close off our most vulnerable side to hunting. The fire was obviously the answer to our fence.

Cavit's first impulse was to jump in and try to fight the fire, but with a big pile of logs alight and flames leaping high into surrounding branches, there was no hope of doing anything bare-handed. I remembered what Fire Chief Hughes had said about telephoning and begged Cavit to drive home. At the cabin I rushed to the telephone while Cavit snatched up tools and sped back to the fire. The operator connected me to our local fire company, which was closer than the state forest fire service. The man on duty said he would contact the service while his own trucks got underway.

Nermin stayed calm as I asked her to be prepared to evacuate. "Get the cats and dogs ready," I said, "and if the fire comes near, let the crows out of the porch. If you get hemmed in, jump into the pond and go far out, or take the other car and just drive away. Meanwhile, stay by the phone in case someone calls for directions."

Grabbing a rake and shovel, I ran through the woods, back to the fire. Cavit was flailing a long-handled shovel in a furious effort to keep the fire from spreading. I joined in, beating the flames with the head of the rake. As soon as some patches were squelched, others flickered up on all sides. The wind drove the flames relentlessly beyond us, and it seemed that the firemen would never come.

We had been working probably ten minutes when our neighbor from half a mile away on another side of the refuge drove up. He did not say how he had found out about the fire; he just grabbed a shovel and set to work. The wind blew steadily, driving the fire further into the refuge in spite of all we could do. Our delaying action did help, however; and when the fire trucks finally arrived, a stream of water soon got the fire under control.

The flames died down and only a smoldering, black area remained. A dozen cars were there by that time, and a gang of men were milling about. There was time to talk, and we found that our neighbor had phoned just after I left the house to warn us of a suspicious-looking hunter he had seen at the corner of our fence. As soon as Nermin told him about the fire, he came right over.

The fire had started in a patch of dry grass just inside the fence, evidently set by a burning match or cigarette tossed through the mesh. Everyone agreed that the fire must have been set deliberately. The bitter cold was unseasonable, and the men shivered in light jackets; soon they had all gone, while we stayed to wait for men from the forest fire service and the state police, who would handle the investigation.

The firemen had probed the piled logs and brush with hooks and saturated the area with water. They had pronounced the fire out but said that men from the forest fire service would come with tractors to plow a firebreak all around, just to make sure.

The man from the forest fire service also probed, found everything satisfactory, and left with the state policeman. Only then did Cavit and I think of Nermin waiting at home, not knowing what had happened, but ready to run for her life. Hurrying back to the house, we found the second car in front of the cabin, packed to the roof with clothing, my typewriter, and a few cherished books. The cats were caged and the dogs were leashed, ready to go. While Cavit unpacked the car, I got breakfast. Nermin had no school that day, but Cavit had to go to work.

With a sinking feeling I saw him drive away, for the day's deer patrol inside the refuge, on foot, still lay ahead. That meant unpleasant meetings with hunters at the borders, risky sneaking about in my own woods, and the torment of hearing shots that signified crippling or death. At ten o'clock I started out, feeling as though a whole day had already passed. Though the fire had been pronounced dead, I felt impelled to inspect the site to reassure myself. Facing the bitter wind, I stepped out of the woods at the end of the deer fence—and discovered a fire in the same place as before. It must have revived from the buried embers. I sprinted home, and calling to Nermin, told her to phone the fire department and then come help me. Throwing tools and pails into the jeep, I drove back to the fire.

It was the dawn fire all over again, but this time I was alone, and my muscles ached from previous exertion. Handling the shovel soon limbered me up, however. Then Nermin was at my side, beating with a rake. I carried water from a ditch 200 feet away and poured it on the outskirts of the fire and into the main blaze where new flames, fanned by the wind, kept sprouting. The fire was contained somewhat by the blackened areas around it, so we had it under control by the time the forest fire service crew arrived. Inspecting the sooty mess, the chief ruled that the fire had reached into deep turf and would require a thorough plowing. We left it to him and his men and went home. It was noon before I could continue my patrol.

The week slowly passed. Each day, as I checked the fence for cuts and kept on the alert for fires, tension mounted. Shots from the adjoining woods echoed widely, making assessment of their location difficult and adding to the uncertainty.

The final day of deer season was Saturday, when Cavit was home to patrol with me. The last shots sounded at 5:00 P.M., soon after the sun had set.

It had been a grim week. Throughout it, I had felt especially close to Grey Owl, whose efforts to save his beavers had met with similar misunderstanding and hostility. On occasion his life too had been endangered, and he had felt the discouragement and doubt which I was feeling. But in spite of all opposition he kept on. I was determined to do the same.

Beavers at Work

"EAGER BEAVER" has become a cliché in our language. But I was to find that, though even a two-week-old kit paddles with a resolute air, the beaver is not the frenetic worker I had supposed him to be. Although there are many tales of beaver industry and his finished works are monumental, I have rarely seen a beaver hurry. The beaver's work record is not achieved by frantic bursts but is piled up, one chip, one handful of mud, one dogged trip at a time. That the results are impressive helps prove the truth of Calvin Coolidge's words: "Persistence and determination alone are omnipotent."

Beaver persistence is a hard thing to beat. An uncle of mine once had a firsthand experience at Whiskey Island in New York State. Beavers had built a dam at one end of a bridge, causing water to back up over the road. Uncle Lewis, who was driving a truck for the township, was sent to salvage the road. "The dam was about three feet high," he told me. "It took me and my helper all day to tear it down. Each stick was woven in so tight we could hardly budge it. Next day my boss sent me up to Whiskey Island to check on the road. There was another dam, only a better one! We worked all that day, taking it out.

"The boss said, 'They won't do it again,' but next day there was a third dam, stronger than ever. We took out five dams in five days. So the boss said, 'We'll try another way.' He had us take electric fencing and put two wires across the end of the bridge. No dams for two days, and then—they made a half circle and went from bank to bank, a very nice job. Finally we made a hole in the middle of the dam and put up the fence again. No more dams."

Some naturalists say that it takes three or four nights for a pair of beavers to build a large, firm dam. At Whiskey Island, no doubt, many hands made fast work; Uncle Lewis had counted twelve beavers swimming around there.

A beaver dam is a solid structure, engineered with skill. The beaver builds it evenly all along its length, using the waterline as a level. For materials he takes what he can find. In rocky country, he may use stones as well as sticks and mud. Where sticks were lacking, a beaver has been known to construct a dam wholly of cornstalks. He curves his dam in the approved hydraulics-engineering manner, its arc convex on the upstream side to give maximum resistance to stress; and he places a spillway at one side.

For a typical dam, the beaver cuts small branches and carries them to the bottom, firmly fixing them with butt ends upstream. He next adds a layer of mud, and gravel and stones if available, which he scoops from the bottom above the dam, then another layer of brush and saplings, and so on. Plastering with more mud, chinking any leaks, he continues until the dam is solid, with a very broad base. Meanwhile, his disturbance of the bottom has loosened materials which the current sweeps to the dam, increasing its effectiveness.

Greenbrier had never built a dam when I was watching. However, once a dam had been built, he maintained it regularly in my presence, often working by day in a steady routine of patrol and upkeep, enhancing his original investment in the thrifty beaver way. Louis Agassiz told of a dam that was discovered when a

Whiskers, showing tail

large pond was drained. It was estimated that the original base of the dam had been laid down by beavers a thousand years before. When undisturbed by man, a beaver pair may inhabit the same water for a lifetime, possibly thirty years, leaving new members of the clan to carry on. They cut many trees, but their food supply is continually being renewed, and only under unusual circumstances would all the food disappear.

Greenbrier held within himself the tools of his trade. In that round head, behind the small blinking eyes, lay sketches of the ideal stream and plans for dam building and beaver housing. There are many records of beavers showing an inborn capacity for dam building. For instance, four orphaned beaver kits, kept overnight in a Canadian cabin, snipped off broom straws and dammed up water that was spreading over the floor from a leaky bucket.

Greenbrier worked with unhurried persistence, as if confidently following a plan. With his nimble black hands he brought up mud from the bottom, pressed out the excess water, and patted it into place with his nose and hands. Often, while carrying sticks and mud in his hands, he would seize one end of a large stick in his mouth, letting the other end trail. Jabbing the stick into place in the dam, Greenbrier would grasp it firmly with his incisors, then ram it home with a powerful twist of his head. He would repeat these downward thrusts many times if necessary, each time getting a fresh grip higher up.

Though his tail looked useless as it dragged like a flap of leather over the ground, it proved to be a handy tool. About fifteen inches long, six inches wide, and nearly an inch thick at the base, it was scaled in a design like that of a pinecone and was naked except for scattered, short, stiff hairs and four or five inches of fur near his body. As he moved up the side of the lodge in his manlike pose, his tail helped balance him and his unwieldy load. His tail also functioned as a brace when he cut trees.

I first saw a demonstration of this latter use of his tail toward the end of the second drought, when Greenbrier and his clan were living far below the main pond. Greenbrier had begun to cut trees for the winter's food supply, and the whole beaver family took keen interest in this chore. Whiskers brought logs, which rumbled hollowly over the dams as she tugged them along. Near the lodge, she dived gracefully with the logs to the bottom of the site which had been selected as a food raft, or storeroom. The water churned and the tapered ends of the logs swayed as she jammed them, big end first, deep into the mud. From time to time she cut off branches underwater, arranging them to fit into the pile.

The young swam about playfully, nibbling on twigs, but never offered to help. In fact, one bold youngster swaggered up to the food raft and snitched a branch. As the work progressed, however, the kits matured; and by mid-October, when they were five months old, they were energetically towing sticks and thrusting them in. So the pantry was stocked with provisions which included poplar, oak, gum, magnolia, cherry, and maple interwoven with long wands of sweet pepper, alder, blueberry, and ilex. Leafy branches fluttered above the surface of the stream, but the bulk lay hidden and preserved, their ends stuck firmly in the mud. A smell like that of ensilage—the odor of pickled bark—hung about the food raft.

I had strolled downstream that particular afternoon to observe otters. I never expected to see beavers at work, since stocking the pantry had heretofore been a nighttime job. Elsewhere, the sun blazed hot above a sizzling world, but here, under dense cedars and massive crowns of maples, was soothing shade, and the water in the pools lay cool and dark. Rounding a curve in the path, I came suddenly on Greenbrier, seated at the base of a five-inch sour-gum tree that was half gnawed through. The tree grew above a steep bank between the path and the stream. I stopped short as Greenbrier, with a start of surprise, wheeled and slid down the bank into the water. As he lay there watchfully, I spoke to him in the coaxing voice he knew. He turned about a few times, looking up at me, his eyes blinking. He did not slap his tail—a good sign of confidence. Then he swam slowly to the edge of the water, climbed back up the bank, and stood beside the gum, still watching me and listening to the reassuring murmur of my voice. Then, only ten feet from me, he settled down to his task.

Cutting the gum tree was hard work, for the wood, unlike poplar, is tough. Greenbrier paused frequently to rest, sitting back on his tail and breathing hard until his spent strength returned. Twisting his head until it was almost upside down so he could bring his built-in chisels into play, he cut above and below the section he wished to remove, then pulled out a chip, and dropped it to the ground. Some of the chips were two inches long. Though the furry folds of his mouth kept most splinters from bothering him, he did sometimes reach with his fingers to pick a fragment of wood from his teeth. It took him half an hour to finish the tree.

In the meantime Whiskers had begun working the stream next to us, pushing sticks to the side and bringing up mud, which she packed in firm wads against the shore. Two kittens had come with her, and they climbed up the bank and scrambled across their father's tail, trying to help him. Greenbrier did not discourage them, though they only got in his way; and they soon left, tumbling down the bank.

With the first creak of the trunk, Greenbrier jerked back to listen, standing erect, his hands curved at his breast. Then he cautiously approached and took another bite. The tree creaked again, giving a little. Greenbrier jumped to one side and waited again. One youngster had crept back up the steep bank just behind his father, who this time hissed a warning, stopping the young one in his tracks.

Little by little, bite by bite, the tree began to lean. When it started to fall, Greenbrier rushed down the bank, shoving the baby before him into the water, where they jostled each other helter-skelter. They circled about for some time, then waddled over a nearby dam and swam away. Whiskers too disappeared. I waited a while, but the beavers did not come back.

The next morning, however, I found the whole family busy at the felled gum, gnawing off bark and chewing leaves. Whiskers gathered many mouthfuls of twigs and carried them into the water to eat, while the youngsters bustled here and there, getting in the way. For three days they came back to the fallen tree. They left only two six-foot lengths—one of them the butt—and these were entirely peeled of bark.

One morning not long afterward, I was surprised to come across nearly a dozen sticks of firewood scattered along the dike. They were actually lengths of magnolia trunk, about four inches thick and eighteen inches long; each was tapered neatly at both ends, with the bark otherwise intact. So strong is our habit of regarding nature as expendable in the interests of man that, without thinking, I gathered the sticks, planning to carry them into the cabin for our little wood-burning stove. I had taken only a few steps when it suddenly occurred to me that perhaps the beavers had cut them for some purpose of their own. I would be stealing from my neighbors. Putting the wood down, I stacked it compactly and resolved to see if the owners claimed their property.

The next day I went back, half hoping that the beavers had left me the wood—perhaps even cut more. After all the food I had furnished them, it did not seem farfetched to imagine that they were trying to reciprocate. The wood was gone, however, and I was glad that I had resisted the temptation to take it. I never found such stovewood again.

One evening in late December, Greenbrier emerged from his lodge, poked his head and shoulders upward, and shattered the thin ice that covered the surface of the stream near his lodge. He started up the channel toward me. First, he poked his nose up, then brought his chin over the glasslike ice before him and pressed

Beaver taking final bites of poplar

down. With a musical clink the ice broke. He moved forward and did the same thing again, widening the channel by six inches as he advanced. In some places the ice resisted, and he would then rise up onto it, head and shoulders out of the water, and bear down with half his weight. Sometimes a great sheet suddenly gave way, throwing him into the water, which of course did not bother him. He came clear up to where I sat on the dam, then wheeled and started back on the other side, cutting another six-inch swathe.

Just then a brown head popped up from among floating ice fragments at the lodge, and Nipper came blustering up the channel. Nosing broken ice aside, he swam toward me and circled in the pool at my feet. Then turning, he paddled after his father, dipping his head in now and then, or reaching over to nibble a jagged edge of ice. Once, close behind his father, he put his small head on the ice barrier and pushed down. When the ice failed to break, he dived in with a flourish, and passing right under his father, came up far ahead in the channel.

Night after night, as long as they could break the ice, the beavers kept the water open. And to my surprise Greenbrier continued working on his lodge. It was during January, in fact, that I decided to try to get photographs of a mud-laden beaver walking up the side of his lodge, a picture I had wanted for a long time. Studying Greenbrier's habits in the previous weeks, I had found him most active a little before midnight.

One night at eleven o'clock, cheered by a bright moon and frosty air and the chortle of flying squirrels cavorting in the tree-tops, I sloshed along the ice-rimmed shore. I took my seat on a pine log twenty feet from the lodge, and with the aid of a flash-light, focused my camera on a point near the tip of the lodge, where I expected Greenbrier, loaded with mud and sticks, to appear. He soon came swimming by me, and circling, regarded me and the camera with suspicion. But he dived into the lodge without slapping his tail. For fifteen minutes I heard muffled gnawing from inside the lodge. Then he reappeared to swim past me upstream toward the dam. The gnawing continued. After quite a wait I heard a crash, which momentarily hushed the twitter of the flying squirrels. Evidently Greenbrier had felled a small tree. It was not long before he came back, entered his lodge, and emerged on the other side. He next made that splashy dive which meant a dip after bottom mud, and I heard the scrape of a branch being dragged up the far side of the lodge. Up loomed a dark blob, beaver-shaped. Quickly snapping the picture, I was completely blinded by the flash, but Greenbrier had not panicked. I could hear him still moving about on top of the lodge. Soon he ambled down the far side and busied himself downstream. I heard a swirling sound as he dived in for another armload of mud and then the steady, hollow tread as he marched once more up the side of the lodge. He came over the peak. I photographed him still on his hind feet, just about to deposit his load. Changing bulbs and waiting again, I caught him next walking up the near side of the lodge with a huge wad of mud clasped in his arms. The moonlight glinted on his wet back and tail.

By that time it was 2:30 A.M. Stretching lame shoulders, I gathered my equipment and walked home through frozen marsh grass sparkling with ice crystals, well satisfied with the night's work.

That weekend, as I gave Al the film to develop, I made a small boast about my beaver pictures.. Al had also wanted the man-with-bundles pose, but he said nothing.

A few days later he phoned. "What setting did you use?" he asked.

"Shutter 125, stopped at f/22," I said glibly.

"How far away were you?"

"About twenty-five feet."

"No wonder they're all blanks," he groaned. "At that distance with a dark object you should have had your lens wide open." There was a long pause. "Live and learn," he said.

I was disappointed, but still the time spent trying to get photos was never wasted.

A week after this failure, the pond and stream were frozen solid except for open water still running over the dams. I had built a blind twenty feet from the lodge, and at dusk one evening, with the thermometer reading eight degrees above zero, I went there to get pictures of a gray fox who passed daily. As I took a seat in the blind, I could hear the groans of ice contracting as the temperature plunged down—violent, ripping noises like canvas being torn by a giant hand. The moon would not rise for another hour.

As darkness settled, the beavers awoke and began talking to each other. A few muffled whines came from inside the lodge, which was sealed by ice, and then a splash sounded as one of them dived down to the underwater food supply. All around the food raft, white bubbles clung to the underside of the ice, the result of the beavers gradually letting out their breath while gnawing underwater.

Because they have unusually large lungs and livers, beavers can work for as long as fifteen minutes underwater, after taking a deep breath before submerging. Flaps close over their mouths, behind their incisors, to keep water from entering. Their valvular ears are sealed, and over their eyes are drawn transparent shields like goggles, thus allowing them to work in comfort. If frightened, beavers have been known to stay pressed flat against the bottom for many minutes.

As I sat huddled in the blind, from the distant woods I heard a soft hoot, which mingled with the beavers' voices. I recognized the cry of the great horned owl. Suddenly a black form moved among the frozen swamp weeds close by. At first I thought it was a fox, but a fox would have drifted like a shadow over the ice. This figure moved in a shambling fashion, and the high hump of his silhouette told me that he was a raccoon.

The moon had risen, and it cast a murky glow. Parting the burlap of the blind, I glanced at the thermometer to find that the mercury had dipped to zero. No wonder the stream was frozen solid to the very lip of the falls. Water still flowed swiftly there, although the channel was getting smaller every moment as the intense cold added layers of ice to its edges. As the moon rose higher, its light cast a path of silver across the black swamp and glittered on the tumbling water. The owl had stopped hooting, and the beaver who had been gnawing under the ice was still. I crouched, rigid as stone, while around me the tortured ice snapped and growled.

All at once I heard something completely unexpected in such bleak surroundings: the joyous voices of young beavers, snug in their winter lodge. Muted by the thick walls, first one melodious tone, then another, reached me. To this duet was added a third voice, then a fourth—vocal music at its best, a quartet humming in exquisite harmony. The sounds carried me in fancy to a springtime orchard, where bees murmured in the blossoms and a warm sun shone. For a few moments I forgot the stark scene before me—the desolate swamp and frozen lodge.

Suddenly turbulence erupted below the dam, and I was startled to see Greenbrier pushing through the water. With a rattle of ice he hauled himself onto the dam. In the dim moonlight he loomed big as a bear. Lowering his head, he began to gnaw; and by the guttural sound of his teeth I realized that he was grinding ice away to keep a channel open, while water swirled black and swift around him, almost washing him off his feet.

It was a moment of vivid contrast—the squat, powerful figure intent on protecting his lodge, where in warmth and comfort his carefree children were singing at their play. For two hours the murmur of the happy youngsters rose and fell like a baby's prattle and never ceased. When I finally took up my gear and crunched homeward, their voices followed me into the night. The fox had not come, my camera had been useless, but my evening was a success.

With the beginning of the February thaw, soon after beaver mating season, Greenbrier started preparing fresh quarters for

Beaver lodge in winter

the coming infants, in spite of the fact that he had worked all winter on the old lodge, his travels making deep grooves in the snow. Only at the top had he refrained from putting mud. He always left a lacework of sticks at the center of the lodge to provide ventilation, and on cold mornings I had seen steam rising from the pinnacle like smoke rising from a chimney.

Why build a new lodge for each batch of kits? We had at first assumed that Greenbrier changed his lodging because of the drought. But a fellow beaver watcher, William Hoisington of New Hampshire, found that his beavers occupied a different lodge each spring. We agreed with him that perhaps a fresh nursery was a health precaution on behalf of the kits.

Greenbrier and Whiskers chose a new site only a stone's throw downstream from the one where they had spent the winter. By mid-April the lodge they were revamping there had risen to a height of five feet, heavily reinforced with sticks and well plastered with mud. From then until the first week in May, I was a daily visitor, teetering on a pine log which jutted above the water from the shore opposite the lodge. I felt like a gossip with a telescope poised at an attic window, shamelessly spying on a neighbor's homelife; but like any gossip, I found an excuse for my inquisitiveness. I wanted to be near when the kittens were born.

The night of May 4, Whiskers did not come for her evening meal at the cove, but Greenbrier made the long journey there and back to the lodge, bringing a supply of poplar for his mate. He took it inside and I could hear the murmur of Whiskers's "thank you," then the crisp sound of her teeth on the bark. Greenbrier emerged again to continue his eternal chores: diving for mud and gnawing on underwater roots, widening and deepening his roadways. For a long time I listened, but no sound of kittens came from within the lodge, so I went home.

On May 5, I was back at the lodge early, perched on the pine log with my feet dangling above the water. Just as it was getting dark, I heard a muffled groan from within the lodge, followed by a faint mew. More tiny voices chimed in, and I could picture plainly the drama being enacted. Whiskers might be taking each kitten in her hands to fondle and brush, and there would be a look of pride in her eyes. Suddenly I heard a mighty groan, as of someone in pain, followed by increased mewing. Evidently another kitten had just been born. Quiet ensued. I climbed down from the log and walked slowly home, recalling the first moments after my own children's births.

One evening shortly thereafter, I sat watching Greenbrier at work while inside the lodge Whiskers nursed the four kittens. I could hear their eager mews. Swimming quietly, Greenbrier dived deep to grub out an old cedar root, which he towed over to the base of the lodge. Then, black tail waving, he made another dive and came up with hands and arms full of mud to reinforce the lodge walls. It was the same old job and the same upright pose.

But now he had a new task, something his recent fatherhood had made necessary. From a dead cedar he stripped off long swatches of bark which he carried into the lodge. There I could hear Whiskers's teeth shredding the bark for the kittens' bedding. This was for their comfort; they did not need diapers, for even very young beavers do not soil their nest. Young and old visit the water, where waste is washed away. The few beaver droppings I have found were like pressed sawdust and had the scent of newly sawed lumber.

The lodge was beautifully landscaped. Red keys of swamp maples made a gay canopy overhead. Rich yellow spears of golden club thrust themselves through the water; later, purple loosestrife would flower from the walls, and buttonbush with its round blossoms and dandelionlike seed heads would flourish. The surrounding moat would bloom with white water lilies—the pads, flowers, and roots of which are so tasty to beavers. Nearby grew broad pastures of marsh purslane, a succulent streamside plant which beavers relish; and the shores were well stocked with water willow, sweet pepper, slender maple saplings, blueberry, and ilex, all together making a rich source of varied foods. Even the algae, which would accumulate later in the summer, would be slurped up by the beavers in strands like green spaghetti.

Sitting quietly on this late May evening, I had a chance to observe some of the beavers' neighbors. As the sun descended and birds hastened homeward overhead, I heard a light splash, and a brown creature about the size of a small cat emerged from the other side of the lodge and swam away. A muskrat, looking like a young beaver except for her pointed nose, closely set eyes, and slender tail wagging behind, had her burrow, with an underwater entrance, in the wall of the lodge. She swam to a tuft of swamp grass and began hungrily nibbling down the fresh spears. Satisfied, she dived, and bringing up a mouthful of tender grass roots, returned to enter her burrow, taking the roots with her. Excited mews greeted her entrance. The cries of the young were higher pitched than those of beaver kittens, befitting the smaller size and more nervous temperament of the muskrats.

All was quiet after the first frenzied greeting; then a small nose poked out of the water on my side of the lodge, and a rat-sized youngster swam toward me. The young muskrat came under my boot soles, and rising in the water, sniffed the rubber. Then he turned away and swam off among the grass and water plants.

As there were few muskrats on our pond, I had been delighted the previous fall to find a characteristic washtub-sized mound of grass and mud heaped in the water near the shore, and to see a half-submerged log littered with discarded bits of stems and roots, showing where a small householder had dined. When ice closed him in and snow covered the mound, I could still see, at one side, a black hole kept open by his breath. Like a beaver, he did not hibernate but sought food all winter, weather permitting. I regularly saw him swimming under the ice or found the pattern of his narrow footprints, with the characteristic mark made by the dragging tail, leading from one hole in the ice to another. Then one day he was gone. Snow had drifted over the opening to his burrow, and there were no fresh tracks leading outward. I wondered if an otter had surprised him far from home and devoured him. There was no sign of vandalism at his home.

Walking nearby a day later, my eye was caught by something high in a tree. Twenty feet up, on a horizontal pine branch, lay what appeared to be a nest or perhaps a furry creature curled motionless among the needles. I had seen squirrels and raccoons sleeping on branches, but somehow this looked different. Could it be a nest lined with fur? My companion that day, a young boy, offered to climb the tree. As he shinnied upward, he shook the branch slightly, and the "nest" fell at my feet. There lay the rear half of a muskrat, which I could identify by its slim, leather-soled hind feet and narrow, flattened tail.

Now, in the spring, I thought again of the little mound builder and of the iron discipline that nature exacts from those who love life. In an unwary moment, he may have shown his brown form against the snow, and a horned owl had grabbed him and eaten one meal, saving the rest. I was glad that at least he had met his end under this stern justice, not meanly in a trap. And I remembered what Ernest Thompson Seton said in his book *Lives of Game Animals*. Seton, who had trapped muskrats as a heedless boy, confined the section "How To Trap the Muskrat" to a single sentence: "I decline to make any statement."

While musing about muskrats, I was watching another tenant of the beaver lodge—a mother tree swallow, whose nest was in a hollow stub jutting among the trees at the lodge center. After lining the hole with wild-duck feathers, the mother bird had laid six white eggs. She and her mate would take turns sitting on them for a period of two weeks. She was perched now at the door of her home, while her mate glided in the air above her, twittering "good night."

The sun went down and a chill settled over the stream. A water

Muskrat at Unexpected Refuge

snake, who had been feeding on insects in the water, came to the edge of the lodge, looked around, then slipped quietly into a hole just his size in the thick dark wall.

Dusk fell and all was silent; the afterglow faded to gray. The male tree swallow left for his roosting place, and his mate withdrew to her eggs. Greenbrier was doing repair work on a nearby dam, and Whiskers and the muskrats were eating among the lilies. Inside the lodge both beaver and muskrat kittens were napping after their meal.

From a tiny crevice near the chimney, a mini-face with beady eyes and quivering whiskers appeared. Out peeked a furry, short-tailed mouse, who looked this way and that, like a man stepping into heavy traffic, before venturing forth. For half an hour I watched her come and go, tugging pieces of dry grass and leaves inside, where muffled squeals told of infants whose bed was being made.

Mentally, I saluted Greenbrier, who, true to beaver tradition, was furnishing homes for a host of other creatures, fulfilling the law of nature embodied in Ralph Waldo Emerson's words:

> All are needed by each one;
> Nothing is fair or good alone.

And then I thought how man, invading the wilderness, flouted that law. "We have heard much of the wonderful intelligence of the beaver," Thoreau wrote, "but that regard for the beaver is all a pretense, and we would give more for a beaver hat than to preserve the intelligence of the whole race of beavers." Beaver hats, I was thankful, were out of style at the moment. I settled down to enjoy the beavers, not knowing what lay ahead.

Getting into the water with the beavers, swimming with them, and sharing in their games was my next goal. I had no idea whether I could do this, yet the parents' trust in me made it seem possible. Anchoring a wooden platform in the stream opposite the lodge, I covered it with burlap and thatched it with grass and dirt. Here I planned to entice baby beavers into my lap and go swimming with them in the moat around Greenbrier's castle. I no longer felt like an intruder and was prepared to meet the latest beaver kittens as soon as they began playing around the lodge.

One afternoon in late June I sat on the platform and waited for them to come. Just before sundown they emerged from the lodge, fluffy and golden brown with appealing bewhiskered faces. At first sight of me, they were immediately afraid and dived back in. When it got darker, they tried again, swimming in circles and gradually coming closer. Finally, as darkness fell, they came up to me and accepted bits of poplar from my hand. But they were suspicious and flighty, diving at the slightest movement. I began to wonder if I could go swimming with them after all. First they would have to get used to me on the platform.

Within a week they were coming out early in the afternoon and swimming right over to where I sat with poplars in my lap. At first, they would climb aboard the platform, sniff at my knee, then draw back hissing. Then several times one or another came as far as my knee without showing fear. At last one got up his courage and clambered over my knee into my lap and sat contentedly munching at the poplar. A sibling scrambled up beside him. As the two greedily stuffed their mouths with leaves, I put one hand on each side of the bolder one and pressed his warm, wet fur. He paid no attention to this gesture, and I knew that he had accepted me as a friend. Members of a beaver family do so much social grooming that they readily accept the touch of a hand, once their initial fear is overcome.

The kittens did not stay long. Even a tiny beaver is not happy long out of water. Before their outer fur had dried, they plopped back in for a refreshing dip. But meanwhile another had come up, and from that time on, my drenched lap was alternately warmed and cooled as one beaver kit after another ambled on or off.

Six-month-old beaver kit reaching for poplar leaves

For a week I let the kittens get accustomed to me. They allowed me to pet them, scratch behind their ears, and even tug them about in the water by their flat tails. Such handling is not unnatural, for the mother beaver holds her young by the tail during the first swimming lessons inside the lodge and thus is able to pull them to safety. Now that the babies were climbing freely in and out of my lap and letting me fondle them, I felt the time was right for my great experiment. The kittens were just about weaned and were swimming in the vicinity of the lodge without parental supervision.

The day I chose to join them in the water was extremely cold for July, and it had drizzled. As I carried poplar to the lodge, the low sun shone through yellow mist. Reaching the platform I called, "Here, Beaver; here, Beaver." Immediately a furry head popped out. He must have been waiting for me. As he lay watchfully on the water, as both young and old do when they first come out, I took off my shirt, laid it on the bank, and stepped into the water, clad in a two-piece bathing suit. I waded to the deep part of the pool where water reached above my waist.

The little beaver had eyed my progress doubtfully from the shelter of a water willow growing on the lodge. As I crouched shivering in the cold stream, he moved forward slowly, raising his head and sniffing in a puzzled manner. About six feet away he dipped in and disappeared, a stream of bubbles rising from where he had been. I wondered if he had retreated to the lodge when I felt a gentle nudge below my knee, then a series of soft taps traveling all the way up my bare leg. The gentle underwater nudgings reminded me of the nibbling of curious minnows, but the beaver's nose, as he explored something new, did not give the sometimes painful nips which the minnows give.

One by one the other young beavers came out and approached me warily, lifting their noses to sniff as they came. With their small black hands clutched against their chests, they teetered on the surface and now and then gave a fishlike flirt with their tails, which propelled them nearer. Gradually, the kittens became bolder until, as one after another reached for the poplar leaves I offered, they grasped my hand in theirs. Sometimes one even held onto my hand as he severed a bit of poplar to carry away. Between bites, they dived and nudged me with tickling noses. Their boldness alternated with sudden spells of timidity, but their fear was similar to that expressed by children playing goblins. It was self-protective, but it had an air of playfulness that was exhilarating.

The kittens' hind legs dangled in the water, and their flat tails were braced on the surface as they clustered around me, eating while I petted them. Now and then one murmured a remonstrance as I held onto a twig too long or a sibling tried to steal a piece that was not his. While I stood there reveling in the babies' antics, suddenly Greenbrier appeared. I had been afraid of his reaction to my stepping into his home pool. Would he tolerate me as a playfellow to his children?

The big beaver swam a little way toward me, then lay quietly in the water with just the top of his head showing. There he stayed, motionless, regarding the feeding kittens and me. For five minutes he watched intently, his expressive eyes showing surprise and uncertainty. Then he floated slowly toward the lodge. He dived smoothly and entered but not before his tail had hit the water with a weak slap. Whether it was a half-hearted warning or an expression of disgust, I could not tell. Perhaps he felt the way some human parents do when a favorite aunt or uncle becomes too popular with their children. He did not come back while I was there.

Although my first "swimming" was mostly a "standing," I was encouraged by the beavers' response and above all by Greenbrier's relatively calm reaction. Unfortunately, work kept me from continuing my experiment that summer. I still have not gone swimming with beavers, but one day I will.

To Save the Beaver

In ADDITION TO WRITING my beaver observations in "Good News," I was now writing articles for wider circulation, and they were appearing in *The Christian Science Monitor* and such magazines as *Frontiers, National Wildlife,* and *Audubon Magazine.* I was also giving lectures at schools and clubs. As a result, I began to receive a lot of mail from people interested in beavers. Some were sympathetic to my views, but others were not. Several breeders sent me literature extolling beaver fur as "The Diamond of Furs" and beavers as "The Empire Builders." From Arizona, Texas, Utah, and Wyoming came enthusiastic letters, enclosing information on a recent breakthrough in successful beaver farming. These brochures expressed a point of view which I tried to understand but could not.

The first sale of beaver skins from the New World was held in 1672, in London, England. At that time the beaver was literally the emblem of gold. Beaver pelts were the coin of the realm for centuries in Canada; and the value of food, clothing, and other items was based on their worth. By 1812, when John Jacob Astor's fur company was making a fortune on beaver skins, the pelts were valued at five dollars per pound. One beaver was worth the equivalent of fifteen mink.

As beavers became scarce, many attempts were made to domesticate them in order to produce ranch furs, as had been done with mink, fox, and chinchilla. Such an attempt was made in 1928 by the Game Division of the Michigan Department of Conservation. Starting with 30 ranches and 1,129 beavers, the project reached a high point of 57 ranches and 1,703 beavers. But the experiment failed. "In theory," Dr. G. W. Bradt wrote, "beaver farming looks like a royal road to riches." But the beavers would not reproduce successfully in small pens, and in large enclosures they did not become sufficiently numerous for a profitable harvest.

The literature of the Empire Builders, noting the failure of early attempts to domesticate the beaver, boasted that they had found a way to succeed where others had failed. They advised potential clients that the price of beaver pelts should go up many times because of domestication and that there was a ready market, as furriers were anxious to buy ranched beaver pelts.

One glowing brochure ended with the pitch: "Start your herd TODAY!" There was a picture to go with it—dozens of tiny pens in which beavers were confined and were to remain until their coats matured and became prime.

Reading these brochures distressed me. I walked to the pond where evidence of beaver life was all around me and thought how much better it was to observe them in their natural homes, watching their actions when they were free and undisturbed. I knew that a beaver could never be happy in a cage.

I agreed with Swedish zoologist Lars Wilsson: "It is really surprising how little we know about the living creatures around us, and our respect and regard for them is in direct proportion to our knowledge."

If the general public knew more about beavers, perhaps their attitude would change. Certainly we knew at firsthand that, to many people, beavers were either simply a nuisance or else, through their pelts, a source of income. We knew that Mike

Deflora, our neighbor, was not alone in his opinions. We had found other traps besides the one on the lodge, but since they were old and rusty we hoped the danger to our own beavers was over.

It was not long after we became friends with Whiskers and Greenbrier that the New Jersey conservation department declared an open season on beavers and otters. This meant that we had to patrol for trappers all during the month of January; for even though our land was posted, making trapping along our stream illegal, there was always danger from poachers, especially during an open season, when the taking and selling of beaver pelts would be within the law.

That year, we could find no signs of trapping within our borders, but we learned later that poachers had caught at least one beaver on our property. We resolved to redouble our patrols the following January, but the conservation department decided to give the beavers a "rest": there was no open season.

Two years later, in June, a small item appeared in our local newspaper. The Fish and Game Council had again declared a one-month open season on both beavers and otters, to begin January first. Since beavers and otters were now our close companions, the thought of their being caught in traps horrified Cavit and me.

I have been told that "you can't fight city hall," but I do not believe it. You can fight, although you may not win. Even a rabbit may become an avenging tigress when fighting for her young; and now, ill-equipped like the rabbit, I lashed out with whatever weapons I could find. I knew I would make mistakes, but I would learn from them.

I began my campaign by writing to the conservation department and the governor and by sending to the New Jersey press a mimeographed release alerting the public to the announced open beaver season and pleading the animals' cause. A few papers published the release, and those stories struck some sparks. I also wrote to everyone I knew in New Jersey and to friends of wildlife in many other states. Scores of people wrote letters to the department; some wrote their local newspapers and the governor. I received word from the governor that the matter was being ably handled by the conservation department, and from the department came a form letter, full of justification for the proposed season. (As far as I could determine, all of us who protested received identical letters.) It said, in part: "A season of this type is brought about by social pressures resulting from citizens of the state who find that beaver and otter are interfering with their desires and represent an economic loss, and they request protection of crops, roads, fish and other items in which they have a major interest. As an example, [the property owners in] the watersheds in Northern New Jersey do not want beaver on their property and insist that they be removed. We know that beaver prevent run-off, are capable of storing water, and furnish habitat for other species of wildlife; however, the water companies complain that the small impoundments caused by beaver raise the temperature of the water, and they deem this to be undesirable. On the other hand, these animals flood cranberry bogs at the wrong time of year, plug up culverts, and interfere with the spillways on lakes, all of which brings many complaints to the Fish and Game Council. . . .

"Just recently, we have been able to capture bear through the use of tranquilizers, and move them to the northwest section of the State where adequate environment exists. We are not able to do this with either otter or beaver inasmuch as wherever we place them in the State at this time they conflict with the interests of people who are extending their living quarters into what was formerly rural areas. . . .

"The Division of Fish and Game and the Fish and Game Council stress the need to protect the integrity of the environment and endeavor to maintain a certain number of these animals so they can be observed by those interested. Any reduction carried out is done in a responsible manner with scientific finesse and with regulations based upon the recommendations of our wildlife biologists. . . .

"The increasing human population in New Jersey and the extension of the residential areas into what formerly was rural, or even wilderness, brings people into conflict with many of our wild animals, and in order to comply with the interests of the citizens, it is mandatory that certain animal populations be reduced to a point where they become compatible with the social demands of New Jersey people."

Not one person out of a hundred in my lecture audiences had ever seen a wild beaver or otter. Now the conservation department asserted that we were being overrun with both these animals and that they had become a menace to human welfare.

I agreed that beavers might be out of place in some situations but failed to see how specific complaints could justify killing them statewide or how trapping for sport could be called "scientific finesse." It seemed to me that their value as water conservators alone far outweighed the damage charged to them. In many instances, roadbeds could be raised, bridges built to arch over a beaver dam, the value of timber or crops balanced against that of a high water table. With millions of dollars being spent annually on education, including museums of natural history where stuffed beavers and otters are displayed, why not spend some money to help preserve these animals alive? I felt that the spread of human population into the beavers' territory was all the more reason why education rather than destruction should be stressed. Instead of continuing to cater to trappers, the department should initiate a program of public education about the benefits of beavers and otters so that there would be fewer complaints.

These points were presented to the Division of Fish and Game. It was all to no avail. The Fish and Game Council, composed of hunters, fishermen, and farmers, had declared the open season, and it would stand. One hundred permits were issued at five dollars each, with the holders privileged to kill five beavers and five otters apiece.

Disheartened, Cavit and I looked to our defenses. The beavers were in the main lodge that summer, in the middle of the big pond. In plain view from our cabin window, they would be fairly safe, and we would watch for any signs of trappers entering the refuge. But it was not to be that easy. To our dismay, we found that Greenbrier was renovating a flimsy, old lodge into a sturdy, imposing castle, and starting the winter food raft adjoining it, in the most vulnerable spot in the entire refuge. The place he chose was far up from the pond, where high ground gave trappers easy access by way of a farm road and a short walk past our gate. For us to reach this lodge would mean an all-but-impossible struggle through 500 feet of slashings, twisted roots, tangled masses of weeds, and clogging water two feet or more deep and bottomed with mud.

"A bridge is the only thing," said Cavit, one day when we had just staggered and floundered our way across the morass, muddy water splashing over our hip boots. "Something like you built out to the lodge to watch the first kittens."

"Yes, but this is much farther and there are no hummocks to build on."

"How about pallets?"

Al had brought us several loads of old pallets, double wooden platforms nailed on opposite edges of short two-by-fours, to break up for firewood; and we had used a few here and there as temporary stepping-stones in marshy places. One pallet is approximately three feet square and weighs about all a man can carry.

"But we'd need dozens." I wished I had not cut up so many to burn. "Maybe we can pick up some broken ones cheap. Let's ask Al where he got his. And how about boards leading between?" I continued. "We could never cut enough logs."

"We'll find some secondhand lumber."

When we told Al, he looked dubious. "That's all I had," he

said. "Somebody gave 'em to me. Don't know where to get more." But he was thinking—so hard that his hand stopped fondling Junior's ears and the little dog had to give him a nudge with his muzzle.

I was not surprised when a few days later Al called up and elatedly cried, "Bonanza!"

"What's up?" I was feeling depressed, for Cavit and I had tried in vain to find pallets.

"We've hit the jackpot! You know the city dump? . . . Well, I went down there to look for hollow logs for raccoon houses, and there they were, just what you need. There's *hundreds* of 'em lying all over."

"Hollow logs?"

"No, no. Pallets! Somebody just dumped a whole gang of 'em, and some are in pretty good shape. You'll have enough to make a dozen bridges." He went on with enthusiasm. "You take my pickup. And I'll go down there noontimes, when I can. We mustn't let 'em get away."

We got the pallets, all we could use. Cavit and I strung a few of them together with scraps of lumber we had on hand, but we needed strong boards. Then Al came through again.

"We've struck it rich!" he announced. "I passed the corner of Seventh Street today, and they're tearing down that old feed mill. There's planks two inches thick on that floor. Go ask about 'em."

The next days were anxious ones, as the slow-moving, slow-talking contractor took his time about dismantling the mill. He refused to accept a deposit on the lumber, and I was afraid that somehow we would miss out. Once before, looking for bird-house material, I had come on an old church being torn down, and the man had promised me all the boards I could cart away. By the time I returned with a borrowed truck, they were being loaded on another man's truck.

"But you promised them to me," I said, flabbergasted.

"Oh, well, you just wanted them for birdhouses," he remarked casually. "This guy wants to build a garage." I was afraid that beavers would not rate any higher than birds, so I haunted the millsite determinedly.

It rained. The contractor was sick. Some of his workmen failed to show up. For nearly a month I hovered about like a vulture awaiting a death. At last the boards were ripped up, and after a nail-pulling party we loaded them into Al's pickup. It took several trips to bring them home, where we piled them close to the swamp. Each board was twelve feet long, eight inches wide, and nearly two inches thick. "They'd hold an elephant," Al said. "And they're wide enough so you can walk easy."

In our spare moments we set to work building the bridge. September passed by, then October. We inched along, snaking around stumps and cutting through half-submerged obstacles, laying track as we went over each hard-won stretch. By mid-November, ice formed on the water at night, and after a few minutes of wrestling the heavy pallets into place, our gloves were sodden with very cold mud. We desperately wanted to finish before deep snow or thick ice could stop us.

At last, late in December, the final pallet was set, the last plank laid. That night it snowed. It was with a deep sense of accomplishment that we looked at the snow-covered path wandering across the swamp. Al gave his seal of approval as he walked through the snow out to the end of the bridge and gazed at the lodge, which lay before him like an enormous dip of ice cream. "Here's the perfect spot for a blind," he said. "I'll make one this afternoon. You can use it for shelter while you're guarding the beavers, and they'll get used to it by spring so we can take pictures. We might even get otters here. 'Aim at the moon, and if you miss you might hit a star.' "

That evening I began my twice-daily vigil, which was to last for nearly three months. I did not trust poachers to stick to the legal one-month season.

When the snow blanket was new, human encroachment could be detected without much trouble; when the snow melted, tracks would be hard to find. But as I was at the lodge morning and evening, I was sure that nobody had come.

One by one, the critical days of January crept by. On Friday of the last weekend, with only four days to go, a light snow fell. No tracks were visible at the dam when I made a careful check that evening, and I left early to attend a meeting.

At five the following morning, I went to the dam, and walking along its crest, came suddenly on a place where the snow had been disturbed. From the far end of the dam, boot prints led to a hole that had been broken in the ice but was now thinly refrozen. There, hidden among a clump of buttonbush stems, a stake had been driven deep into the dam. A frosty chain disappeared into the black water. *What would I find at the other end?*

Gripping the chain with both hands, I pulled with all my strength. It held fast. Was Whiskers or Greenbrier lying unconscious or lifeless at the end of the chain, a fifty-pound deadweight? Frantic, I angled the chain and pulled again. It gave a little. Then, bracing my feet on the slippery logs, I slowly hauled it up, a blind fury of hate mixed with sorrow giving strength to my arms. Whatever was at the end was concealed by the dark water.

Just then I heard the door of a pickup slam. Someone had come to the farmer's field outside our gate and would be here in a few minutes. I must see if what I held was alive. With a final heave I brought a big old-fashioned leg-hold trap to the surface. Two cement blocks, which were grating together, had been wired to the trap. Gripped in the steel vise were two toes of a beaver's hind foot, a fragment of torn web clinging to them.

I dropped the trap back into the water, and the heavy blocks sank with a gulp. Springing across the dam, I hid in the brush behind a pine trunk—just in time. A man appeared in the dim light of predawn, striding swiftly through the snow. I was not prepared for what I saw next. Stepping in the man's footsteps, hurrying to keep up, came a boy of about twelve, well bundled against the cold. The man was Mike Deflora and the boy was his nephew.

"Uncle Mike! Wait!" the boy cried in a loud whisper, his breath clouding the air.

"Sh-sh-sh!" Mike warned him. "We gotta hurry. Gotta get out of here before day."

There was still no hint of daylight, but the white snow gave reflected light. My heart beat fast, pounding into my throat. Holding back, I waited to see what they would do.

Mike strode to the trap and gave a tentative yank on the chain. "I think we got one," he told the boy. "Feels like a big one, too." In spite of his age he was stronger than I, and he pulled the trap out of the water without trouble. "Dad-blast it!" he exclaimed with surprise. "Could've swore we had one. It got away. Looka this!"

The boy had come up beside him, and he leaned over to see the trap. "We did get one!" he said eagerly. "Look at those claws. Can I have 'em, Uncle Mike?"

"Sure, Roy. Nice trophy for you. Here, I'll wedge the trap apart and you take 'em out."

As they were about to confiscate part of Whiskers's body (we learned later that it was Whiskers who had been caught, but she did not hold it against us), I stepped out from behind the pine. "Well, Mike. . . " I croaked.

He wheeled with the agility of the woodsman, while the boy straightened up with a frightened gasp. For a moment we just looked at one another, each trying to master his own emotions and plan what to do next. In the faint snow light, Mike's faded eyes showed a mixture of fear and bravado; I saw no trace of shame. His nephew Roy stood, head down, scuffing the snow.

"Just tendin' my trap," Mike said then, throwing his head back defiantly.

"Did you catch anything?" I asked.

"No, ma'am," he said, aggrieved. "Caught one, but it got away. Left its claws in the trap."

"Did you set any other traps here?"

"No, ma'am, just this here. Well, guess I'll be goin'." He started to bend over the trap.

"Please leave the trap there," I said. "It's sprung and it won't hurt anyone now. Come up to the house and have a cup of coffee. My husband's there. Let's talk things over."

We trudged Indian file along the creaking boardwalk, and nearing the cabin, saw the first light of day creeping up in the east. Cavit, who had just returned from patrolling the east end of the refuge, was in the kitchen when we walked in the door.

"Sit down, Mike," I said. "Roy, take off your things while I make you some hot chocolate." Lamely, I played the role of hostess.

Mike acted the nonchalant guest. "Thank you, ma'am," he said, and taking off his hat, sat down at the table. Roy slouched into a chair and looked guardedly around the kitchen.

Cups clattered on the table; the refrigerator door slammed shut; the teakettle began to hiss. "Help yourself," I told Roy and passed the cream to Mike. What a bunch of hypocrites! I thought to myself. Here we are acting the gracious hosts when we would rather be strangling someone, while Mike is playing the humble guest of folks he tried to rob. Above all I seethed at the humbug of a civilization in which fur wrested from friendly animals is prized as a status symbol.

With all the activity going on, nobody had to speak. But now that we were drinking our coffee, something had to be said.

"What happened?" said Cavit.

"Ask Mike," I mumbled.

"Oh, I set a trap at your dam," said Mike. His hand trembled as he buttered his bread. "Didn't get nothin'."

"Why did you do it?" Cavit asked sternly.

Mike looked up, then back down to his plate. He took a big bite of bread and began chewing. We all waited. Roy's eyes traveled from one face to another.

Mike spoke. "Well, you had beavers, and you didn't want 'em. The state opened a season. They're fair game."

"But you walked right by our signs to set your trap!" said Cavit. "Didn't you see the signs?"

"Yeah, I seen 'em. But signs don't give you the right. Them beavers belong to the trappers. Our license pays for 'em. Besides, they was goin' to waste. What good's a beaver to you?"

Cavit was saved from answering just then, for a tap came at the door. It was Al, who had planned to get snow pictures while shadows were long.

He joined us at the table, and sizing up the situation, sat quietly sipping his coffee.

Mike's question hung in the air, asking for an answer which somehow we could not give. The old trapper spoke a language long outdated, and it would take a new language to express what we felt about beavers. Into my mind flashed a picture of my husband's Turkish parents, whose lives were restricted because they were unable to adjust to the modern alphabet when it replaced the ancient Arabic characters in use when they were young. We live by the language we learn, I thought, and Mike had been taught only the glory of the kill. But there sat Roy beside him. Roy could learn something new.

"Did you ever see a beaver?" I asked.

"Not a live one." Roy wiped a line of chocolate froth from his lips and scratched his ear. "I seen a pelt once. Joe Brasco had it."

"Did you like the fur?" I asked.

"Yeah, it was all right. But I'd rather see the whole beaver."

"Why do you suppose a beaver has such a thick, soft coat?"

"To keep warm, I guess. That water's cold."

"Good point! That water *is* cold, and the beaver, otter, and mink who live in it grow dense waterproof fur. You should see a beaver sitting up, grooming his fur. He puts oil on it just like you oil leather boots. Only in this case he's waterproofing *himself*."

"Then the water can't get to him," Roy said, sitting straighter.

"That's right. He moves through water like you do in insulated boots."

"Gee! Have you seen a beaver close up like that—oiling himself?"

"Yes. Do you have a dog?" I asked.

"Yeah."

"What's his name?"

"Hotshot."

"I bet you love him."

"Of course. Everybody loves his dog."

"That's the way I love beavers." I turned to Al. "Got your camera?" I asked. As Al went out to his truck, the rest of us moved into the living room, where Roy perched on the edge of a cushion and Mike settled down on the couch.

"You think the beavers are going to waste," I said. Going to a file, I pulled out a sheaf of beaver photos.

Mike and then Roy looked at them one by one. "That one'd go fifty pounds," I heard Mike mutter. Once he glanced up and said, "How'd you get so close? Them things slap their tails and dive if you get anywhere near 'em."

"Does your dog run away when you come near?" I asked him.

"Gee, they're keen pictures," said Roy. "I didn't know you could get that close to a wild animal. How'd you do it?"

Al had stepped back into the house, his Hasselblad resting on the curve of his hand. "With this," he told Roy, tapping the camera with his finger, "and with this," indicating his forehead.

"Boy, I wish someone'd show me," Roy said wistfully. "I thought the only way to see a beaver was to trap one."

"Oh, you don't want to do that," said Al, shaking his head. "A beaver's got feelings, just like you. I used to hunt animals; didn't know better. Now I hunt with a camera."

He began to show Roy the camera, explaining about the lenses. He was slowly building up the boy's interest, just as he had done with me. As I watched the enthusiasm grow in Roy's face, feelings of anger and frustration left me. In their place came words of Dr. Albert Schweitzer, which I knew by heart but sometimes lost sight of. "When in spring the withered grey of the pastures gives place to green, this is due to the millions of young shoots which sprout up freshly from the old roots," he had written, speaking of our moral awakening.

I looked at the dry, harsh root that was Mike Deflora, already withering away, clinging to his old life to the last; and I felt only pity for him. I looked at Roy and remembered the crowds of youngsters I had met in schools, who, when asked if they loved animals, raised their hands vigorously. There were millions like them, I realized, springing from the ancient ways—green, fresh, and unspoiled.

Al and Roy were hovering over the photos, and Al's teaching instinct was strong. "We'll get better ones next spring," he was saying. "Get a camera and I'll take you out with me. Okay?"

"Yes sir," said Roy. He and Al shook hands.

When Mike got up to go, we regretfully warned him that we would have to take legal action if we found him in the refuge again.

Up to that time we had depended on the good will and honesty of the local people, however much their philosophy might differ from ours. But traps deliberately set inside our borders showed us that we might have to resort to more than warnings. We hoped Mike had learned his lesson, although we somehow doubted it. But we had given Roy something new to think about, and that made the incident worthwhile.

Man Versus Animals

As "PROTECTORS of the Beaver People," Cavit and I rejoiced that Whiskers had escaped death or serious injury, but we were not content to preserve one beaver family and one small patch of woodland from exploitation. We longed to see all beavers protected.

Soon after Whiskers's narrow escape, we became aware that other people were concerned about the plight of beavers and were working for the same goal as we, in their own parts of the country and in their own way. Among them was Carl Marty of Wisconsin, called "the Saint Francis of the North Woods," who had raised orphan beavers and otters and was working to get both species protected before they became extinct.

With the help of Minnesota otter expert Emil Liers, Marty and his colleagues succeeded in getting the otter trapping season closed for one year, and two wilderness counties kept it closed for a second year. But the strong trout lobby succeeded in opening it again.

Marty was fortunate to receive support from Alvin E. O'Konski, United States representative from Wisconsin, whose remarks in the *Congressional Record* of June 18, 1968, stirred nationwide interest in Marty's work.

Another active champion of beavers and otters in Wisconsin was Paul Munninghoff, a former trapper. Public reaction to his articles, which appeared in the local papers in 1969, helped bring needed pressure to bear, and the beaver and otter seasons were closed a month earlier that spring. One of his pleas that was particularly eloquent said in part:

"Some of you who read these lines will have been fortunate enough during your stay in our north country to have seen an otter gliding along the banks of one of our rivers or lakes. Or you may have had him pop up in a span of bluegill decoys on a frosty morning in October, snorting and blowing, and making a fuss about the intruders in his territory.

"If you were this fortunate, mark it well in your memory. Because you won't see him again, and it's possible that not even your growing sons will see him or any of his relatives. His pelt is on a stretching board, and it will put $17 or $18 in some trapper's pocket.

"And if you've marveled at the hydraulic engineering skills of the family of beaver who built the dam that you took your sons to see, mark *that* well in your memory, too. They're gone. And their pelts will bring an average of about $12 to some trapper."

Beaver Bill Hoisington was fighting the beavers' cause in New Hampshire, and in several other states animal lovers were taking up the fight. The courage of these men was an inspiration to Cavit and me. Spurred by their example, we considered what steps we ourselves could take to prevent another open season on beavers and otters in New Jersey. How could we arouse public opinion?

As it turned out, public opinion was already being aroused. Under the auspices of the Humane Society of the United States, an antitrapping campaign was launched in 1969 by two energetic women of northern New Jersey, Mrs. Thomas Maxwell and Mrs. George Thomas. Although their campaign had little to do with beavers and otters specifically, it would benefit them indirectly by focusing attention on the suffering caused to animals by the widespread use of traps.

Mrs. Maxwell's first encounter with trapping had come a few years before, when some boys on their way to school tried in vain to beat a trapped raccoon to death, then left him there, intending to kill him after school. Mrs. Maxwell's father, who owned the adjoining property, found the raccoon and released him.

Later, when Mrs. Maxwell read a newspaper article extolling fur trapping in the suburbs as a wholesome hobby for boys, she called on the editor, taking along a trap which she had removed from a pet cat's foot. She told him about other cases of pets being mutilated and of Canada geese and other wildfowl found with feet mangled or missing as a result of coming in contact with traps. The editor was shocked and agreed to run an article exposing the cruelties of trapping.

Mrs. Maxwell began to read everything she could find on trapping, including material by the trappers themselves. When she learned that the nearby town of Montclair already had a restrictive trapping ordinance in effect, she secured a copy. One of her county freeholders became interested in her crusade, and upon studying the Montclair ordinance, sent copies to all seventy mayors and town councils in the county, requesting that they consider passage of similar ordinances.

Meanwhile, Mrs. Maxwell and another investigator came up with nine verified reports of trapped pets in their own community of Oradell. They presented the evidence to their town council, which passed a restrictive ordinance. Several months later Mrs. Thomas succeeded in getting a total ban on trapping in her neighboring town of Oakland.

Not content with the progress in their own communities, both women enlisted the help of clubs, church groups, youth leaders, and councilmen in other northern New Jersey areas to begin

Raccoon

getting local ordinances passed and to support a state bill, drafted by their senator, which would restrict the use of leg-hold traps and control trapping throughout the state.

While the antitrapping campaign continued in high gear, our refuge environment was threatened from a new quarter. The township was going to widen Unexpected Road, and the county was to put in a new bridge where our stream crossed the road below the refuge. With misgivings I noticed that, instead of using new dirt on the road, the township crew worked with bulldozers to push the dirt already there to either side. This meant that the road, which had served as a high dike between a swamp below and a shallow pond above, would be in danger of being flooded should the beavers build a lodge and raise the water level on the refuge side.

I had heard of beaver colonies being eliminated if their dam-building activities interfered with roads. I did not want that to happen to our particular beavers. If beavers could not live freely in the refuge, where *could* they live? And with a new bridge in the offing, here was a chance to have it built so that the beavers might coexist with man.

A township official promised that the road would be raised and that the new bridge would not interfere with the beavers. I assumed that he would notify me when a bridge committee met, so I could present the case for our beavers.

The days went by and I heard nothing more. Then I happened to meet our county freeholder in charge of roads and bridges. "Your township man wrote me," he said. "Everything'll be okay. We have a new kind of gate, all aluminum, so you can arrange water level to suit yourself."

"It's not up to me," I told him. "It's up to the beavers. What if they clog up the gate?"

"Don't worry," he soothed. "The water level will be high. They won't interfere with it."

More time passed. On the first day of May I was in the woods when I heard a metallic rumble coming from Unexpected Road. My first thought was that someone was dumping more trash along the road in a place we had just cleaned up. Or could it be the utility company beginning to install the electric line they had promised? Then I remembered the bridge! Hurrying down there I found that a county road crew had just unloaded lengths of thirty-six-inch, corrugated aluminum culvert and was preparing to demolish the old bridge. Already they had torn out Greenbrier's dam under the bridge, thereby draining the marsh so that a dozen muskrat houses were stranded above water.

Appalled, I asked the foreman, "Is this the kind of 'bridge' you're using? The freeholder promised me something that the beavers wouldn't interfere with." Gesturing toward the twin culverts I declared, "That's just the kind of thing beavers jam full of sticks; then they won't be allowed to stay."

"I've got a job to do, ma'am," the man said, his face seamed and weathered like granite. "I've got my orders." He strode to the side of the bridge and looked down at the current flowing beneath.

"But the freeholder promised. . ."

"Can't help that. I get my orders from the county engineer. Got orders to put this here culvert in." Wheeling, he started toward his truck.

Hurrying to keep up with his long strides, I pleaded, "Please wait until I can call your boss. Maybe he doesn't know about the beavers."

"No time," he said brusquely. "Come on, now. You're holding up six men and all this equipment." A huge crane with a bucket had come rumbling down the dike and was standing ready.

Desperate, I kept on. "I don't care. Once the wrong bridge is in it'll be too late. Give me your boss's number then, so I can call him, or let me get in touch with the freeholder. He promised. . ."

"That don't matter," he cut in. Then he yielded a little. "I'm going to talk with the assistant boss now. I'll ask him about it."

He jumped into his truck. Starting the motor, he activated the radio and began a conversation of which I could hear only his side. "All set here," he reported crisply. "Water's down and we're putting 'er in. . . . What trouble? . . . Okay, I'll be right there!" He gave me an irritated glance, then addressed the mike again. "There's some woman here says the freeholder promised some kind of bridge for the beavers. Wants to know something about it." He got his answer and shut off the radio.

Jumping out of the cab, he started walking rapidly toward the workmen. "Trouble over at Number Four," he shouted to his assistant. "Boss wants me there right away. Carry on here."

"What did your boss say?" I asked.

"He said, 'Go ahead and get the job done.' "

"Can't you do something?"

"Ma'am, I'm busy. Beavers don't worry me. I got bridges to build." He leaped into the truck, grabbed a scrap of paper, and scribbled a name and phone number. "Here," he said, handing it to me, "You call the engineer if you want to." He revved the motor and backed away.

I felt like a fool as I turned home. How did I think I could buck the system? Bravado faded away, and in its place came a feeling of lassitude and defeat. But the thought of the beavers and their helplessness strengthened me. I started running home.

The engineer was not in his office, and his assistant knew nothing, brushing me off with a fast bit of patter. But he said he would try to contact the freeholder and ask him to call me. I then phoned a civil-engineer friend who owned land downstream from Unexpected Road. He and his sons had been delighted when one of Greenbrier's dams below the bridge made an ideal swimming pool for them, and they looked forward to having young beavers move down into their woodland. They were ready to make any concessions necessary so that a colony could exist there.

He suggested that I phone Trenton and talk to the head of the Control Section, Water Policy and Supply Council, Department of Conservation and Economic Development, to find out if the county had permission for the twin-culvert structure. If they did not, we might stall them until the situation could be reviewed.

The Water Policy and Supply Council told me that they were leaving the whole thing up to the county, and they seemed as unconcerned about the beavers as had the road crew.

Next I phoned Beaver Bill in New Hampshire for advice. He recounted the latest episodes in his running feud with authorities there, as he tried to keep his beaver family from being ousted by state officials because the persistent animals were clogging up the dropbox at a culvert. The box had been installed so water level in the pond would remain high for the benefit of fish and game, but the beavers, stimulated by water running into the box, kept trying to fill the box with mud and sticks. Once a week Hoisington had to drag out the accumulated debris with a clam rake. Otherwise he would lose his beavers, in spite of the fact that they had become celebrities since the ex-governor's granddaughter had taken up beaver watching.

I was not cheered to find that a man with such famous beavers was having trouble protecting them. Then the freeholder called to say he was coming to the refuge to talk things over. All the time I could clearly hear the clang and rumble of the bridge gang, which gave a painful sense of urgency to the situation.

When the freeholder came in the early afternoon, he reiterated his assurance that all would be well. As before, he pointed out that a new-type gate would be installed, so that if water rose too high, the level could be lowered. But that was just what I was afraid of. What if the beavers built right over the gate, making it inoperative? What would happen to them? Just that morning I had heard one of the road crew mutter, "If the beavers flood the road, they'll have to go. They cause maintenance problems." There seemed a spiteful note to his voice.

Our freeholder, however, was an unusual man, a nature lover with a wildlife refuge of his own, on which he had spent thousands of dollars and much work. He promised that if the beavers did mess up the new culverts, he would be responsible for taking action to help them. With this assurance I had to be content.

Two days later came a letter from our civil-engineer friend. He had talked with Trenton himself. The head of Control Section, Water Policy and Supply Council, had advised us to keep a close watch on the culverts; and if they proved to be a problem over the next year or so, we should make a formal complaint to his office. They would then investigate and order the county to install a larger culvert if necessary. In addition, our friend had talked with the freeholder, who had vowed that, if required, he would place a semicircular row of pilings against which the beavers could build, letting the water flow over to enter unobstructed pipes. He had ordered the men to place the culverts unusually high, so that water could rise to a high level before entering them at all.

That summer, which was among the wettest in history, extensive flooding occurred in New Jersey. On Unexpected Road water on the refuge side, upstream from the culverts, came surging back, drowning the muskrats' homes, which were above the water level since the marsh had been drained by the removal of the beavers' dam under the bridge. Then flood water filled the inadequate culverts, and still rising, burst through the roadbed at its weakest point, cutting a deep channel right across the road. Unexpected Road remained closed for many weeks, while the former pond was only a sea of mud with a creek flowing through it.

In the fall the roadbed was raised, the small culverts were lowered, and a third was installed along with them. A thin film of water covered the mud around the remnants of the muskrat houses. Whiskers, Greenbrier, and the current batch of kittens were still with us; but Greenbrier did not rebuild the dam which before had kept water high and had allowed the excess to flow over and go under the old bridge. Now water flowed through the skimpy culverts with little held in reserve.

It was disheartening to realize that I had been of no help to my beaver family in this particular instance. In effect, I had stood helplessly by while a dam was torn out and a pond destroyed. I felt bad about the muskrats, who had just begun to come back after our eight years of protection. I realized that one voice was not enough. This conviction was strengthened later when I read about a group of angry nature lovers in Alabama who visited their county commissioners and persuaded them to change plans and raise a roadway rather than lower a beaver dam when floods threatened to overflow the road. Changing official decisions could be done. But I knew of no group in our community big enough or concerned enough to do the job.

Epilogue

"LET'S GET OUT OF HERE," Cavit said to me one morning. "Let's go somewhere and find some real wilderness where we won't have all this trouble."

It was December. The deer season had just ended. It had been a particularly harrowing time for us, and we were weary and depressed. Our run-ins with hunters had been often unpleasant, even ugly. We had been threatened, and just the day before someone had fired a large-caliber bullet at close range into our mailbox, tearing holes two inches across through the metal sides.

Now for the first time, Cavit was discouraged enough to think about pulling out.

"But what about the beavers?" I asked.

"We'll take them with us. We'll go where the streams aren't polluted, where there are mountains and tall trees and no hostile people."

"You won't find things better somewhere else," I said, though I felt myself weakening. Our position did seem futile, yet I hesitated to abandon Unexpected. I had the feeling that if we did, we would desert our new post also should things get tough.

Small-game season was still on, and that day as I patrolled the refuge, I wondered if I could say good-bye. Skirting swampy

171

places where tree swallows nested each summer, I walked along trails shared by raccoons and foxes, and through weed-grown fields where bluebirds and indigo buntings would be coming back in the spring. A covey of quail sprang up and sailed away over a multifloral hedge. They were the ones hatched in a nest I had found that spring and were reared in this very field. Could I turn Unexpected over to become a hunter's paradise or a developer's dream?

All day I tried to make a decision. I went back over what we had done and tried to do. All had come to a dead end. Our plea in Trenton had failed; our lives were threatened; people around us resented our stand. At last I assented to Cavit's idea of taking our beavers and going with them into the wilderness, far away—and safe.

That evening I sat down beside the cove, and Whiskers came over to me. She looked up with a happy murmur as I handed her a twig. I saw her as she had appeared in the summer against a backdrop of mossy logs and dark shadows pierced by the bright flame of the prothonotary warbler, while her kittens frolicked around her. Looking at her fat, humped figure, small blinking eyes, stubby black hands, and absurd frog feet, I realized how much I loved her. How could I exile her from home? Yet there seemed no other solution.

A few days later, when I was looking up something in *Bartlett's Familiar Quotations,* I came across a particularly apt saying by George Bernard Shaw:

> People are always blaming their circumstances for what they are. . . . The people who get on in this world are the people who get up and look for the circumstances they want, and, if they can't find them, make them.

Circumstances were all against the beavers, I knew. Their only hope lay in the creation of something new. Since there was no group large enough to help them, why not form such a group? Beaver Bill's motto is: "A beaver is to befriend." I added a corollary: "A beaver is to *defend*." Thus The Beaver Defenders was born, with a bold, prophetic: "They shall never be trapped anymore."

I designed a letterhead, planned posters, and sent news releases nationwide. People from many states and Canada began to join. In my lectures I started telling more stories of beavers and making a plea for their protection, and several persons in each audience asked to become members.

Cavit, who had been regretting his momentary defeatism, joined in my decision to stay, and we faced the future together. We agreed that Unexpected and the beavers were worth any hardship. And we vowed never to rest until the motto of The Beaver Defenders became a reality.

Beverly Bernstein, a teen-age member who had visited Whiskers and Greenbrier and their family, expressed her feelings and ours in the following verse:

> I watched them splash and swim about,
> Diving once more from shore.
> And in my heart beat a swift refrain—
> *They shall never be trapped anymore.*

NOTE TO THE READER

The Beaver Defenders is open to all persons who will pledge themselves to do something creative to help beavers. For more information, write to:

The BEAVER DEFENDERS
Unexpected Wildlife Refuge, Inc.
Newfield, N.J. 08344

PRINTED IN U.S.A.